The Apostolic Faith Mission in Zimbabwe Split: Unveiling How the Loser Lost

Jaison Ndlovu

Published by Jaison Ndlovu, 2024.

While every precaution has been taken in the preparation of this book, the publisher assumes no responsibility for errors or omissions, or for damages resulting from the use of the information contained herein.

THE APOSTOLIC FAITH MISSION IN ZIMBABWE SPLIT: UNVEILING HOW THE LOSER LOST

First edition. September 3, 2024.

Copyright © 2024 Jaison Ndlovu.

ISBN: 979-8227533586

Written by Jaison Ndlovu.

Table of Contents

DEDICATION

To my daughter, Lomalinda Grannie Ndhlovu, whose inspiring idea ignited this journey. To my sons Logic Amos, Eureka Eulogy, Russell Hillary and Elisha Heritage, not forgeting their sister, Misery, whose unwavering support and material assistance fueled its progression. To my spouse, Susan Ndlovu (nee Mahogo), whose genuine interest provided constant motivation. And to my dear mother, Resiya Magundwane, (nee Chikwinya), whose prayers guided every word written. To my grandchildren who I have always wanted to know and tell when I am gone. Last but not least, all my relatives. This book is a testament to the love, encouragement, and unity that has always surrounded me.

CHAPTER one

The AFM in Zimbabwe River of Change

Since the official formation of the autonomous Apostolic Faith Mission in Zimbabwe in 1983, following its separation from the Apostolic Faith Mission of South Africa, the organization has experienced several breakaways. Historically, these breakaways have been characterized by a simple separation, where the departing group would merely "pack its bags and go," without causing significant disruption to the parent organization.

However, a recent event in 2018 marked a departure from this trend. A faction within the organization attempted to oust the sitting Executive, leading to a massive split with far-reaching consequences. This split had the potential to cause a ripple effect, leading to divisions within the Apostolic Faith Mission in various countries. While the physical structures and assets of the organization remained intact in some countries, allegiances were divided, with some individuals and groups sympathizing with the pro-reformist faction, while others aligned themselves with the anti-reformist faction.

This recent development highlights the complexity and depth of the challenges facing the organization. The labels "pro-reformist" and "anti-reformist" suggest that the split was driven by fundamental differences in vision, values, and approach to governance. The fact that alliances were formed across national boundaries indicates that the issues at stake were not limited to local concerns but resonated with members in other countries. This situation presents an opportunity for the organization to engage in introspection, dialogue, and reconciliation, with the aim of restoring unity and promoting a shared vision for the future.

The primary obstacle hindering reconciliation is the distinct nature of the recent split compared to previous breakaways. Historically, breakaway groups have followed a charismatic individual who became the founder and leader of the new church. In contrast, the recent split is characterized by a collective leadership, with the Apostolic Council at its helm. This council comprises the executive, provincial overseers, the Bible College principal, and heads of various ministries, such as Welfare and Evangelism.

This Presbyterian system of governance, where decision-making authority is distributed among a group of leaders, presents a challenge for negotiations and reconciliation efforts. Unlike churches led by a single individual, where the ultimate decision rests with that person, the Apostolic Council's collective leadership requires a consensus-driven approach. This makes it more difficult to engage in negotiations and reach a unified decision on reconciliation, unless the council as a whole decides to rejoin the other faction.

The complexity of this governance structure is further compounded by the need for consultation and agreement among council members. In contrast, individual-led churches can navigate reconciliation talks with greater ease, as the decision-making process is more streamlined. The Presbyterian system, while promoting a more collaborative and representative leadership, creates a more intricate landscape for reconciliation efforts.

The history of the Apostolic Faith Mission (AFM) in Zimbabwe is largely a reconstructed narrative, pieced together from recorded interactions between the Church and government authorities. Unfortunately, the South African archives of the AFM of South Africa, which oversaw the Zimbabwean mission field until 1983, contain limited unbiased records. The available historical accounts primarily focus on the native church of the AFM in Zimbabwe, which was operated by black Africans, under supervision of the white men.

However, it is essential to acknowledge that a parallel, whites-only church existed in Zimbabwe, led by white missionaries. This aspect of the Church's history appears to have been intentionally erased or removed from the records. Despite the existence of separate church buildings for whites in various cities, the history of this white-led church remains largely unknown.

The absence of records and the focus on the native church's history create an incomplete narrative, obscuring the complex dynamics of the Church's operations in Zimbabwe. It is crucial to recognize the dual nature of the AFM's presence in Zimbabwe, with both black and white congregations existing simultaneously, yet with distinct histories and experiences. Uncovering and acknowledging this erased history is essential for a comprehensive understanding of the AFM's past in Zimbabwe.

In this narrative, we will focus on the native church, which evolved from the Apostolic Faith Mission (AFM) of South Africa to the AFM in Zimbabwe. The whites-only church, which remained under the AFM of South Africa, did not merge with the newly formed black-led AFM in Zimbabwe in 1983.

Following Zimbabwe's independence in 1980, black people, including non-AFM members, began attending services at the previously whites-only church auditoriums. This was a symbolic act of defiance and a assertion of their newfound freedom after years of oppression and segregation under the white-led government. As a result, many white members stopped attending church services, fearing potential reprisals from the newly empowered black majority.

By 1983, when the Zimbabwean chapter of the AFM of South Africa gained independence and formed the AFM in Zimbabwe, only a small number of white members remained. This marked a significant shift in the demographic makeup of the church, reflecting the broader societal changes taking place in post-independence Zimbabwe.

The formation of the AFM in Zimbabwe was a milestone in the church's history, signifying a transition from a South African-led mission to a locally led and governed church. This development was a response to the changing political landscape and the need for the church to adapt to the new realities of an independent Zimbabwe.

Following Zimbabwe's independence in 1980, the black leaders of the native church navigated the transition with strategic caution. While they had been advocating for independence from the South African-led mission, they refrained from openly expressing their demands to the masses. Instead, they skillfully negotiated a seamless handover takeover ceremony with the South African representative and Rev. Edgar Gschwend, the Mission Director.

This calculated approach ensured a smooth transition, avoiding potential conflict or disruption to the church's operations. However, the underlying dynamics were more complex. Many white members had already left Zimbabwe, either voluntarily or due to the changing political climate, while others had stopped attending church services altogether.

The departure of white members and the decline in attendance were likely influenced by various factors, including:

1. Political uncertainty: The transition from a white-led government to a black-led one created uncertainty, leading some whites to leave the country.

2. Fear of reprisals: Some whites may have feared potential reprisals from the black majority, given the historical context of oppression and segregation.

3. Changing social dynamics: The shift in power dynamics and the emergence of black leadership may have made some whites feel uncomfortable or unwelcome in the church.

Despite these challenges, the black leaders of the native church successfully navigated the transition, paving the way for the formation of the Apostolic Faith Mission in Zimbabwe in 1983. This marked a significant milestone in the church's history, as it gained autonomy and began to forge its own path under local leadership.

In this discussion, we will focus exclusively on the splits and breakaways within the native church, now known as the Apostolic Faith Mission (AFM) in Zimbabwe, since its independence in 1983. We will not delve into the history or dynamics of the whites-only church, as it operated separately and distinctly from the native church, despite sharing a common name and head office.

The native church and the whites-only church existed in parallel, with minimal interaction or overlap. Therefore, we will not consider the whites-only church as a breakaway or split from the native church. Instead, we will examine the breakaways that have occurred within the black-led AFM in Zimbabwe since 1983.

These breakaways have resulted in the formation of new churches and denominations, often led by charismatic individuals or groups seeking autonomy or expressing dissent with the AFM's leadership or doctrine. We will explore the historical context, causes, and consequences of these breakaways, as well as their impact on the broader Christian landscape in Zimbabwe.

By focusing on the splits within the native church, we can gain a deeper understanding of the complex dynamics and challenges faced by the AFM in Zimbabwe, as well as the resilience and adaptability of its leadership and members.

Unlike the Apostolic Faith Mission of South Africa, which successfully merged its four previously segregated churches (whites-only, Indian, mixed race, and blacks) into a unified organization with a single constitution and leadership panel, the Zimbabwean chapter failed to achieve unification. In fact, the concept of unity was never realized in Zimbabwe, as the whites-only church and the native church operated in isolation, with minimal interaction.

The only white individuals who engaged with the native church were missionaries, who served as intermediaries between the two separate entities. There was no direct interaction or collaboration between the whites-only church and the native church. This lack of unity and cooperation can be attributed to the Apostolic Faith Mission of South Africa's reluctance to relinquish control over the mission field in Zimbabwe.

Ironically, the Apostolic Faith Mission in Los Angeles, whose Apostolic Faith Missionaries founded the South African chapter, never exerted ownership or control over the AFM in South Africa. This highlights the inconsistent and complex dynamics at play within the organization. The failure to achieve unity in Zimbabwe can be seen as a missed opportunity, and the legacy of segregation and separation continues to impact the church's history and development.

The Apostolic Faith Mission (AFM) of South Africa's Zimbabwe chapter faced rejection from the white community from its inception. The pioneers of AFM in Zimbabwe were marginalized immigrant workers from Matabeleland South, including general hands, gardeners, cooks, housemen, farm, and mine workers, who introduced the AFM message in December 1908 and officially in 1915. White missionary Dugmore arrived later, following reports of numerical growth in Zimbabwe (then Southern Rhodesia).

Interestingly, when white individuals in Southern Rhodesia joined AFM, they affiliated directly with the Johannesburg church, bypassing Dugmore and other white missionaries. Little is known about these white AFM members, but their presence was evident. They attended services in separate churches, with only their nannies and cleaners allowed on the premises, but not inside the church building. Black men were restricted to cleaning and gardening roles, excluded from the church building.

As a result, AFM of South Africa in Zimbabwe was perceived as a predominantly rural, white-led church, with separate churches for whites in Harare, such as Waterfalls, Kopje, and Avondale. However, the truth is that the church, as it is known today, was always black-led, with white overseers. The separation between black and white congregations was evident in the use of facilities like Rufaro Conference Center and the Bible College, which were initially built for black students in Gillingham (Dzivarasekwa), a black township, and not accessible to white members.

However, the recent independent church, the AFM in Zimbabwe, failed to evangelize and integrate diverse groups, including whites, contributing to this perception. The church's inability to bridge this divide and evangelize across racial lines is a missed opportunity for unity and growth. Despite this, the AFM in Zimbabwe remains a vibrant, black-led church, with a rich history and heritage.

Although the church has experienced breakaways, it has also successfully nurtured both pastors and congregants to establish separate ministries and churches, often unknowingly. While breakaways can be as painful as childbirth, they can also be as beneficial as the new life that follows. Just as newborns grow and become parents, reproducing and expanding their family, breakaway churches can grow and flourish separately from their former church, carrying the DNA of their origins with them.

This process is reminiscent of Jesus' instruction to his disciples to wait in Jerusalem for the Holy Spirit. After Pentecost, the Apostles didn't immediately recall their commission to "Go and make disciples..." and instead stayed in Jerusalem until persecution scattered them to various places, where they began ministering in ways they couldn't have while still gathered in Jerusalem. This dispersal allowed them to spread the gospel and establish new communities, just as breakaway churches can lead to the growth of new ministries and congregations.

Healthy church growth can manifest in various ways, and breakaways may be viewed as an opportunity for new chapters or denominations to emerge. Just as parents may experience their children leaving the family home in different ways, church leaders may see members depart to form new congregations.

Consider the analogy of parents with three daughters, each leaving home in a unique manner. The first daughter may bring her partner into the family home, leading to a hasty departure due to unexpected circumstances. The second daughter may follow traditional courtship and wedding customs, receiving a formal sendoff. The third daughter may elope, returning only to introduce her parents to their new grandchild.

Despite the varying circumstances, all three daughters are now building their own lives, married and thriving in their respective homes. Similarly, breakaway churches or ministries may arise through expulsion, formal separation, or voluntary resignation. Ultimately, these new entities can still grow and flourish, contributing to the diverse tapestry of Christian communities.

In God's eyes, the motivations and methods behind breakaways may be secondary to the outcome – the expansion of His kingdom and the spread of His message. By embracing this perspective, church leaders can focus on nurturing their remaining flock while acknowledging the potential for growth and renewal in unexpected places.

CHAPTER two

Tributaries of Truth and Growth

Consider a scenario where the Apostolic Faith Mission (AFM) in Zimbabwe had remained unified since 1983, without any splits or breakaways. It's unlikely that the church would have achieved the same level of growth and expansion it has experienced over the past forty years. The absence of splits would have meant that the church's growth would have been contained within its existing structure, potentially limiting its reach and impact.

In this hypothetical scenario, it's unlikely that the church could have accommodated its current membership in a single conference center. The sheer number of congregants would have required a massive venue, far exceeding the capacity of most conference centers. Moreover, the pastors who broke away from AFM would not have had the opportunity to build their own churches and ministries, which now boast thousands of congregants.

The reality is that when pastors are not part of a larger, established church, they are motivated to work harder to grow their own churches and ministries. This drive leads to innovative outreach, evangelism, and discipleship efforts, resulting in numerical growth. However, it's essential to acknowledge that every new church or ministry has its roots in the main church, either directly or indirectly. No church is an island; they are all interconnected and part of the broader body of Christ.

The splits and breakaways that have occurred within AFM in Zimbabwe have, in fact, contributed to the church's overall growth and expansion. While they may have been painful and challenging at the time, they have ultimately led to a more diverse and vibrant Christian landscape in the country.

The widely accepted perspective is that a river is formed through a complex interplay of geological processes, including water accumulation, where precipitation, snowmelt, or groundwater seepage collects in a low-lying area or depression, such as a valley or basin. This accumulation of water can occur through various mechanisms, including precipitation, snowmelt, and groundwater seepage.

As the accumulated water begins to flow downhill due to gravity, it creates a small stream or rivulet. This initial flow is driven by the slope of the land and the force of gravity. As the water flows, it erodes the surrounding landscape, creating a defined channel or path. This process is facilitated by the abrasive action of sediment and rocks carried by the water.

Smaller streams and rivers join the main channel, increasing its volume and flow. This process, known as tributary capture, can occur through various mechanisms, such as headward erosion, where the main river's flow erodes the banks and captures smaller streams, or avulsion, where smaller streams are diverted into the main river due to sedimentation or tectonic activity.

The river continues to erode its banks and bed, carrying sediment downstream and depositing it at its mouth or along its course. This process shapes the river's channel and surrounding landscape. Tectonic activity, volcanic activity, and human activities, such as river engineering, dams, and channelization, can also significantly impact a river's course and flow.

Understanding these processes is essential for managing and conserving rivers, as well as predicting and mitigating the impacts of natural and human-induced changes on these vital ecosystems.

Additionally, rivers are typically identified and named based on their source, rather than their mouth. The source of a river is considered the point of origin, where the river begins its journey, usually located at a higher elevation such as a spring, mountain, or hill. This is where the river's name is usually applied, as seen in the example of the Amazon River, which is named after its source in the Andes Mountains in Peru, rather than its mouth in the Atlantic Ocean in Brazil.

Identifying a river by its source helps define its watershed or drainage basin, determines its flow direction, and establishes its unique identity and characteristics. In contrast, the mouth of a river, where it empties into another waterbody, is not typically used as the primary identifier. While the mouth is an important feature of a river, it is secondary to the source in terms of naming and identification.

This approach to naming rivers based on their source provides a clear and consistent way to identify and distinguish between different rivers, and helps to understand their unique features and characteristics.

Is the way we identify and name rivers based on their formation and source necessarily the absolute truth, or is it simply a human construct and a matter of convention? In other words, is there a more fundamental or objective reality to the nature of rivers that goes beyond our arbitrary labels and classifications?

Is the notion that a river originates from its source the ultimate truth, or is it merely a perspective based on our observation of the river in its mature state, without witnessing its formation and growth?

To gain a better understanding, let's examine the Jordan River by tracing it backwards from its outlet in the Dead Sea to its source.

The formation of the Dead Sea, also known as the Salt Sea, can be attributed to its location in the Rift Valley, a region of intense tectonic activity. The most logical theory is that the movement of the Earth's crust created a depression, which eventually became the Dead Sea, a long time ago. In this sense, this depression was formed as a result of the Arabian Plate moving away from the African Plate, creating a rift zone.

As precipitation continued to fall on and around the formed depression, surface water began to erode the sides of the gigantic gully, creating little streams that flowed into the depression. Over time, these tiny streams grew and merged, with the most prominent one capturing other tiny tributaries through headward erosion. This process formed the Jordan River, which continued to extend its course through headward erosion and tributary capture until it reached its present source.

This process illustrates the concept of stream capture, where smaller streams are captured by larger ones, eventually forming a river. Precipitation at the highest ground elevation causes surface water to flow following gradients as flow paths, with larger paths capturing smaller ones, until a stream captures the accumulated flow, eventually being captured by a river itself, until the flow reaches the sea or ocean.

The headward erosion and tributary capture processes are essential for the formation of rivers and streams. Without these processes, some surface water would end up in gullies, disused mines, and other depressions, never reaching the sea. For headward erosion or tributary capture to occur, there must be a larger channel at a lower elevation first, creating a gradient for the water to flow.

New rivers can indeed form through headward erosion, where the river's source moves upstream due to erosion, extending its length and potentially creating a new breakaway angle from the original inflow course. This process can lead to the formation of a new river or a significant change in the existing river's course.

Tributary capture can also lead to the formation of new rivers or significant changes in the existing river's course. When a smaller stream is captured by the main river, it can experience increased flow speed and volume, causing it to grow in both width and length. This can lead to the development of a new tributary or a change in the existing tributary's course.

Tributary capture can occur through various mechanisms, including:

The main river's flow erodes the banks and captures the smaller stream.

The smaller stream's course changes due to sedimentation or tectonic activity, causing it to flow into the main river.

The main river's flow diverts the smaller stream's course, capturing its flow.

These processes can lead to the formation of new rivers, changes in river courses, and the creation of complex river networks.

Observing the growth of a city can provide valuable insights into understanding the development of a river. When entering a city like Harare, you're typically greeted with a welcome sign, which has progressively moved further away from the city center over the years. Initially, the sign was around ten kilometers from the center, but as the city expanded, it was relocated to fifteen kilometers, and now it's situated about twenty kilometers away. This illustrates how cities grow outward from their initial core, with the center becoming more refined and developed, while the perimeter expands.

Similarly, a river's growth can be viewed through this lens. As a city's outskirts stretch further, a river's length expands from its source, with the source shifting further away from the mouth. Despite this, the river's water still originates from its source and surrounding catchment area, flowing downstream. This parallel highlights the dynamic nature of both city and river growth, where expansion and development occur simultaneously, shaping the landscape and ecosystem.

Just as a city's infrastructure and beauty evolve over time, a river's course and characteristics change, influenced by geological and environmental factors. By recognizing these similarities, we can deepen our understanding of the complex relationships between a river's source, growth, and surrounding environment.

Here, we're drawing analogies between the growth of rivers and cities to understand the growth and development of the church. Just as God created a fixed amount of water that circulates through various forms - clouds, seas, oceans, groundwater, and human-made containers - the church, founded by Jesus Christ, has a fixed foundation, but its expression and reach can expand and change.

The water that precipitates at the source of a river is not new; it's recycled water, just like how the church's growth is not about creating new foundations but about expanding and branching out from the original source. The largest river in an area has its tributaries, and those tributaries have their own smaller branches, just like how the church has its main branches and smaller denominations or breakaway groups.

In the context of the Apostolic Faith Mission (AFM) in Zimbabwe, we see a similar pattern. The AFM, like many other denominations, has its roots in the original church founded by Jesus Christ, and over time, it has grown and branched out, giving rise to various breakaway groups, including the recent 2018 split. These breakaway groups, though separate, are still connected to the main church and its leaders, just like how tributaries are connected to the main river.

This analogy highlights the organic and dynamic nature of church growth, where new branches and expressions emerge while remaining connected to the original source. Understanding this process can help us appreciate the complex and ever-changing landscape of the church, just like the ever-flowing and changing course of a river.

The Apostolic Faith Mission (AFM) in Zimbabwe, established in 1983, has a rich and complex history that spans over a century. While it operated as the AFM of South Africa from 1915, its roots can be traced back to the church founded by John Graham Lake, Thomas Hezmalhalch, and others in 1908 in Johannesburg, South Africa. This church, in turn, was an extension of the Apostolic Faith Mission founded by William Joseph Seymour in Los Angeles in 1906, which was a key movement in the Azusa Street Revival.

Furthermore, the AFM's emphasis on healing ministry can be attributed to the influence of John Alexander Dowie's Zionist movement, which emerged in the late 19th century. Dowie's movement emphasized the importance of faith healing, and his teachings had a significant impact on the development of the AFM's doctrine and practices.

In this sense, the AFM in Zimbabwe cannot deny its roots in these earlier movements, which have shaped its theology, practices, and mission. The church's history is a testament to the dynamic and evolving nature of Christian movements, where ideas, influences, and leaders intersect and shape the course of the church's growth and development.

By acknowledging its roots in these earlier movements, the AFM in Zimbabwe can gain a deeper understanding of its own identity and mission, while also recognizing its connection to the broader Christian tradition. This awareness can foster greater unity and cooperation among different Christian denominations and movements, including the several that broke away from the AFM in Zimbabwe, as they recognize their shared heritage and common goals.

There have been several breakaway groups from the Apostolic Faith Mission (AFM) in Zimbabwe that have chosen to affiliate with other churches or ministries, adopting a godfather-godson relationship. This affiliation has led to a complete disassociation from AFM in Zimbabwe, attempting to erase the memory of their origins from their new converts. However, while this may alter their narrative, it cannot erase the reality of their history, which will continue to shape their identity and inform their decisions throughout their existence.

These breakaway groups may attempt to rebrand and redefine themselves, but the legacy of their past remains an integral part of their DNA. The relationships they form with new affiliations may bring new influences and perspectives, but the roots of their origin will always be a part of their story. This is similar to how a person's upbringing and family history continue to shape their life, even if they choose to distance themselves from it.

The reality of their past will continue to impact their present and future, influencing their theology, practices, and culture. While they may try to suppress or deny their origins, the truth of their history will remain, waiting to be acknowledged and reconciled. Ultimately, embracing their true identity, including their complex history, can lead to greater authenticity and integrity in their ministry and relationships.

The mother church, Apostolic Faith Mission in Zimbabwe, attempting to discredit breakaway churches by labeling them inaccurately will not be productive. In God's plan, everything is designed to bring Him glory. This situation is akin to a church auditorium reaching maximum capacity, prompting expansion or extension, rather than allowing the overflow to establish their own church with their own pastor. This mindset echoes the Tower of Babel, where humans tried to control and manipulate God's plan, leading to division and confusion.

This approach goes against God's design, as seen in Zechariah 2:4, where it is written, "Jerusalem shall be inhabited as towns without walls, because of the multitude of men and livestock in it." This verse illustrates God's desire for His people to expand and grow without artificial boundaries or constraints. Trying to measure and contain Jerusalem, or in this case, the growth of the church, goes against God's plan.

Instead of embracing the natural growth and expansion of the church, some leaders try to control and manipulate it, leading to breakaways and division.

This stems from a desire for power and control, rather than a willingness to let God guide and direct His people. By attempting to measure and contain the church, leaders risk repeating the mistakes of the past, where human pride and ambition led to chaos and confusion. Ultimately, God's plan will prevail, and His glory will be revealed through the growth and expansion of His Church.

Just as a main river acknowledges and respects its tributaries, recognizing the valuable contributions they make to its growth and abundance, a thriving city welcomes the inputs and diversity of its outskirts, leading to a richer and more vibrant community. Similarly, God blesses and enriches the mother church for giving birth to new churches, just as a mother is blessed by the arrival of new life.

However, just as a natural birth is preferred over a Cesarean section, which is often a result of an overdue or complicated pregnancy, we should strive for organic growth and development in our churches. Instead of forcing or manipulating the process, we should allow for natural expansion and multiplication, trusting in God's timing and plan.

A natural birth symbolizes a healthy and thriving ecosystem, where growth occurs effortlessly and harmoniously. In contrast, a Cesarean section, while sometimes necessary, can represent a more contrived or forced approach. By embracing the natural order of growth and development, we can avoid unnecessary complications and trust in God's sovereignty, allowing our churches to flourish and multiply in a healthy and sustainable way.

The scriptures we read today have stood the test of time, enduring for millennia due to their authenticity and unwavering truthfulness. Similarly, if both the Apostolic Faith Mission (AFM) in Zimbabwe and its breakaway churches were to chronicle their histories with unflinching honesty, future generations would inherit a precious legacy of transparency and integrity. By doing so, we would be following the example set by the Bible, which candidly records both the triumphs and shortcomings of God's people.

The Bible's unvarnished account of human failings and divine interventions serves as a powerful testament to its authenticity. It presents a nuanced and realistic portrayal of history, eschewing the temptation to gloss over or distort facts for the sake of appearances. In like manner, if we, as believers in the Bible, were to commit our stories to paper with equal sincerity, we would bequeath to our descendants a rich tapestry of truth, woven from the very fabric of our experiences.

By embracing truthfulness in our record-keeping, we would demonstrate our commitment to the values embodied in Scripture. This approach would foster a culture of accountability, humility, and trust, allowing future generations to learn from our successes and setbacks. In doing so, we would honor the legacy of the Bible and its unwavering dedication to truth, ensuring that our stories, like those of old, would endure for generations to come.

We are grateful to the Lord for the recent split in the church, which has been the most publicized and legally authenticated division in our lifetime. This event has allowed us to witness and recount most of the events as they unfolded, providing a unique opportunity to document historical truths. Unlike previous splits, which may have had hidden agendas and unclear motivations, this recent division has been marked by transparency and clarity, revealed directly or indirectly. Moreover, it has been characterized by the shortest period of numerical growth, allowing us to observe and learn from the process in real-time. This split serves as a valuable case study, enabling us to understand the complexities and challenges of church divisions and the subsequent growth of new ministries.

CHAPTER three

The Complexities of Breakaway Ministries

To grasp the subtle distinctions between the splintering of the Apostolic Faith Mission of Zimbabwe from the Apostolic Faith Mission in Zimbabwe, it's essential to examine two pivotal breakaways that significantly impacted AFM in Zimbabwe. While several other splits occurred, the departures of Pastor A V Marufu in 1993 and Pastor Emmanuel Makandiwa in 2010 had far-reaching consequences, sending shockwaves throughout the entire AFM organization.

Pastor A. V. Marufu, alongside his then-wife Joyce, now Apostle Joyce Gombami Marufu, founded Awake Grace Ministries in 1993 in Gweru, Zimbabwe. Pastor Marufu, a charismatic and fearless speaker, was known for his revolutionary mentality and uncompromising stance. He sought to challenge the status quo within the Apostolic Faith Mission (AFM) in Zimbabwe, which he perceived as having adopted a compromising attitude from fearful white missionaries.

These missionaries had altered the original non-racial stance, healing, and prophecy-enhancing teachings of John Graham Lake to conform to the oppressive laws of South African apartheid and Rhodesian segregation. Pastor Marufu's bold approach was seen as a threat by the AFM leadership, who had grown accustomed to the existing system.

As a former cadre, Pastor Marufu was undaunted in his pursuit of truth and justice. His message resonated with those seeking a more authentic and empowered expression of their faith. However, his uncompromising stance ultimately led to a rift with the provincial leadership, resulting in his expulsion or resignation – the circumstances of which remain unclear.

This pivotal event marked a significant turning point in the history of AFM in Zimbabwe, as Pastor Marufu's departure, with thousands of AFM in Zimbabwe sympathetic and vigilant followers, paved the way for the establishment of Awake Grace Ministries. Under the leadership of Apostle Joyce Gombami Marufu, the ministry has continued to thrive, embodying the revolutionary spirit and fearless approach that defined Pastor Marufu's tenure.

When Pastor Marufu left, he was followed by a substantial number of former congregants from AFM in Zimbabwe, although the scale of this exodus was not as extensive as the one that occurred in 1943, when Isaac Chiumbu departed from the Apostolic Faith Mission of South Africa's Zimbabwe mission field, taking a larger group of followers with him. Nevertheless, the number of congregants who followed Pastor Marufu was substantial enough to send shockwaves through the Midlands Province, prior to its subsequent division into five distinct provinces within the Midlands Region.

As soon as Pastor Marufu departed, the national leadership faced a daunting challenge: finding a suitable replacement to revitalize the dwindling congregation at Mkoba 9 Assembly in Gweru. After careful consideration, they identified Pastor Choto, then serving at Mabvuku-Tafara Assembly in Harare, as the ideal candidate to fill the void left by Marufu. With his exceptional leadership skills and charisma, Pastor Choto was transferred to Gweru with immediate effect.

Pastor Choto's impact was profound, and he quickly proved himself to be an able successor to Marufu. His dynamic leadership and vision resonated with the congregation, and he soon became a leading figure within the church. In recognition of his exceptional abilities, Pastor Choto was elected Overseer of Midlands South Province, defeating the seasoned Rev. Salatiel Gwanzura, son of the renowned Samson Gwanzura of the legendary Gwanzura Brothers.

However, as Pastor Choto's fame grew, so did his ambition. He began to pursue his own path, eventually leaving AFM in Zimbabwe to establish a new ministry. Unfortunately, his new venture failed to replicate the success he had achieved under the AFM banner. The ministry struggled to gain traction, and Pastor Choto's reputation suffered as a result. He became another example of a breakaway leader who, despite initial promise, failed to sustain momentum and ultimately faded into obscurity.

This turn of events serves as a poignant reminder that even the most gifted leaders can falter when they fail to listen to God's guidance and instead rely solely on their own judgment. As the Bible cautions, "Pride goes before destruction, a haughty spirit before a fall" (Proverbs 16:18). Pastor Choto's story serves as a cautionary tale about the dangers of unchecked ambition and the importance of humility in leadership.

In contrast to the seismic impact of Pastor Marufu's departure, Pastor Choto's exit from AFM in Zimbabwe has largely faded from memory, leaving no lasting sting. This is surprising, given that Pastor Choto was one of the most dynamic and charismatic pastors in Zimbabwe, renowned for his exceptional leadership skills and vision. During his tenure in Gweru, he demonstrated remarkable prowess in rebuilding and revitalizing the congregation, ultimately surpassing the influence of Pastor Marufu's outfit.

Pastor Choto's achievements in Gweru were a testament to his exceptional abilities, as he successfully rebuilt and expanded the church, leaving a lasting legacy. However, his subsequent departure from AFM in Zimbabwe has been met with a collective shrug, with little fanfare or lingering impact.

Meanwhile, Pastor Marufu's Awake Grace Ministries has continued to thrive, relocating its headquarters and Bible College to Kadoma city. This move has enabled the ministry to expand its reach and influence, solidifying its position as a major force in Zimbabwe's religious landscape.

The disparate reactions to the departures of these two influential pastors serve as a fascinating case study in leadership dynamics and the fleeting nature of fame. While Pastor Marufu's exit left an indelible mark on AFM in Zimbabwe, Pastor Choto's departure has been met with a surprising lack of fanfare, despite his significant contributions to the church.

This dichotomy highlights the diverse roles that pastors play in the kingdom of God. Some are called to revitalize and strengthen the evangelistic efforts of an existing denomination, while others are destined to pioneer and lead a new gospel ministry or church, with Jesus Christ as the supreme head.

In this context, Pastor A. V. Marufu exemplifies the former, functioning like a solar panel that receives direct illumination and power from the sun

(God). He channels this energy to empower others, much like a solar panel energizes batteries and appliances. Marufu's connection to God is unmediated, allowing him to flourish independently.

On the other hand, Pastor Choto's ministry is akin to a battery that relies on an intermediary (the solar panel/AFM) to receive power from the sun (God). His calling is to pastor within the framework of a visible church, leveraging the resources and support of the denomination to fulfill his mission.

This distinction explains why some breakaway ministries prosper while others falter. The battery (Pastor Choto) may mistakenly assume it is the primary source of power, overlooking the essential role of the solar panel (AFM) in recharging it with divine energy. In contrast, the solar panel (Pastor Marufu) effortlessly harnesses the sun's power, requiring no intermediary.

This analogy underscores the importance of understanding one's divine calling and functioning within the designated role. While some pastors are equipped to thrive independently, others require the support and structure of a larger organization to fulfill their ministry. Recognizing these differences is crucial for success in the kingdom of God.

The allegory of the air force pilot further illustrates the distinction between Pastor Marufu and Pastor Choto. Just as the pilot is referred to as the "commander" of the aircraft, regardless of whether they are alone or accompanied by a crew, Pastor Marufu can be seen as the "commander" of his ministry.

Like the pilot, Pastor Marufu is in command of his spiritual aircraft, navigating, communicating, and executing the mission objectives set by God. He is responsible for the safe operation of his ministry and the success of its mission, relying solely on his expertise, training, and authority as a spiritual leader.

In contrast, Pastor Choto's role is more akin to a co-pilot or crew member, relying on the support and guidance of the larger denomination (AFM) to fulfill his mission. While he may have played a crucial role in the success of AFM, his departure from the denomination highlights his dependence on the larger organization.

The title "commander" acknowledges Pastor Marufu's autonomy, expertise, and authority as a spiritual leader, underscoring his ability to thrive independently. Just as the pilot in command is responsible for the success of the mission, Pastor Marufu's leadership and vision have enabled his ministry to flourish, even in the absence of external support.

Following in the footsteps of Pastor A V Marufu's groundbreaking departure, which led to the establishment of Awake Grace Ministries International, another prominent figure, Pastor Emmanuel Makandiwa, now widely recognized as Prophet Makandiwa, also made a significant breakaway from the Apostolic Faith Mission in Zimbabwe.

Pastor Emmanuel Makandiwa, also known as Shingirai Chirume, was born in December 1977 in the Muzarabani district of Mashonaland Central Province, Zimbabwe. His parents, who are elders in the Apostolic Faith Mission Church, played a significant role in shaping his spiritual journey. From a young age, Makandiwa was exposed to the teachings and values of the AFM Church, which laid the foundation for his future calling.

Makandiwa claims to have received a vision from God, calling him to deliver his people from the bondage of Satan. This divine encounter would become the driving force behind his ministry, and we have no reason to doubt the sincerity of his claims. Before partnering with local AFM pastors in Zimbabwe, Makandiwa and his parents organized gospel crusades in 1995, preaching from their home and spreading the message of salvation to their community.

In pursuit of formal theological training, Makandiwa enrolled at Living Waters Theological Seminary, an AFM pastors' training center in Zimbabwe. He graduated in 2002 after completing a three-year program, equipping him with the necessary knowledge and skills to effectively minister to his congregation.

Makandiwa's initial pastoral career began as an intern and probationer, assisting seasoned pastors in Matabeleland. During this period, he worked closely with Pastor A Madziyire, who would later become the president of the Apostolic Faith Mission in Zimbabwe for five consecutive three-year terms until November 2018. This mentorship played a crucial role in shaping Makandiwa's pastoral approach and leadership style.

Following his ordination, Makandiwa was assigned to pastor in Shangani, where he began to make a name for himself as a dynamic and Spirit-filled leader. In 2004, he was transferred to How Mine, and subsequently to Chitungwiza, which was under Mashonaland East Province at the time. It was during this period that Makandiwa's reputation as a powerful preacher and healer began to spread, attracting large crowds and earning him recognition within the AFM Church and beyond.

During his tenure at Hebron Assembly in Chitungwiza, Pastor Makandiwa embarked on an innovative initiative, launching a lunch-hour fellowship at the Anglican Cathedral in Harare in August 2008. As the fellowship grew, it eventually moved to the City Sports Centre. In 2010, he founded the United Family International Ministries (UFIM), a move that would ultimately lead to a divergence from his parent church, the Apostolic Faith Mission (AFM) in Zimbabwe.

As Pastor Makandiwa's focus shifted towards UFIM, his official congregants at Hebron Assembly began to feel neglected, citing infrequent communion services and a perceived lack of attention from their pastor. The AFM constitution did not provide for the type of ministries Pastor Makandiwa had established, which created tension between him and the church leadership. While there were other evangelistic ministries within AFM, such as those led by Pastors Mukwaira, Chiweshe, and Masiyambiri, these were sanctioned by the AFM leadership, unlike Pastor Makandiwa's UFIM.

The unresolved issues culminated in Pastor Makandiwa being indirectly asked to choose between UFIM and AFM. Some attribute his expulsion from AFM to disagreements over the source of his healing powers, but this was not the primary issue. The AFM constitution could not be amended to accommodate Pastor Makandiwa's unconventional approach. However, the name "United Family International Ministries" suggests that Pastor Makandiwa had a long-standing vision, which he pursued despite the constraints of the AFM framework.

In hindsight, it is clear that Pastor Makandiwa needed a launching pad for his ministry, and AFM provided the necessary foundation. As he grew in influence and vision, it became apparent that he could not be contained within the traditional AFM setup. With faith as his guiding principle, Pastor Makandiwa took risks, made disciples, and eventually, in 2010, established a thriving ministry that transcended his AFM roots.

The ministry of Pastor Emmanuel Makandiwa, subsequently known as United Family International Church (UFIC), experienced remarkable growth and expansion, becoming one of the largest charismatic and Pentecostal organizations in the Harare Metropolitan Province. Beyond Harare, UFIC also established a notable presence nationwide, with smaller but significant assemblies scattered across Zimbabwe.

While the details of UFIC's growth and development are not the primary focus here, it is essential to acknowledge its significance as an offshoot of the Apostolic Faith Mission in Zimbabwe (AFM). UFIC represents the second major split from AFM, following Pastor A V Marufu's departure in 1993 to form Awake Grace Ministries.

The emergence of the United Family International Church (UFIC), as a distinct entity from AFM underscores the dynamic nature of religious movements and the complexities of leadership and vision. Pastor Makandiwa's ministry, with its unique blend of charismatic and Pentecostal teachings, resonated with a significant segment of Zimbabwe's Christian population, leading to the establishment of a thriving and influential church.

The analogy of the solar panel and the sun is once again evident in the context of breakaway ministries. Unlike Pastor A V Marufu's and Pastor Emmanuel Makandiwa's ministries, which thrive independently like solar panels harnessing direct sunlight, other breakaway ministries like Pastor Chipunza's School of Deliverance and Pastor Vutahwashe's Heartfelt resemble batteries that rely on an intermediary source of power. These ministers, though genuinely called and empowered by the Lord, attempted to operate autonomously without the necessary qualifications, forgetting their designated role as batteries requiring recharging from the external source (AFM).

During their tenure within AFM, their preaching attracted overflowing crowds in various traditional venues, demonstrating their potential. However, upon disconnecting from the external source, their ministries began to show signs of fatigue, struggling to sustain momentum. If not reconnected to the recharger (AFM), they risk eventual decline, potentially damaging their reputation and impact.

This phenomenon highlights the importance of understanding one's divine calling and functioning within the designated role. While some ministers are called to be solar panels, directly harnessing God's power, others are meant to be batteries, relying on an intermediary source for recharging. Recognizing this distinction is crucial for

maintaining vitality and effectiveness in ministry.

This development highlights the evolving landscape of Zimbabwean Christianity, marked by the growth of new movements and the diversification of religious expression. As we explore the historical context of these events, we gain insight into the complex interplay of factors that shape the trajectory of religious organizations and the leaders who guide them.

Within the Apostolic Faith Mission (AFM) in Zimbabwe, there existed a remarkable preacher, Pastor P D Chiweshe, whose impactful word ministry earned him widespread love and respect from diverse audiences. His influence extended to over half of Zimbabwe's population, either through live attendance or audio media. Despite his exceptional gift, Pastor Chiweshe humbly recognized his role as a "battery" - a vital component, but one that relies on an external power source.

Unlike Pastor A V Marufu and Pastor Emmanuel Makandiwa, who successfully ventured into independent ministries, Pastor Chiweshe wisely acknowledged his limitations. He understood that his strengths lay within the framework of AFM, where he could flourish as a "battery" recharged by the organization's support and structure.

Had Pastor Chiweshe attempted to replicate the autonomous path of Marufu and Makandiwa, he might have faced significant challenges, potentially leading to disappointment and unfulfilled potential. By embracing his designated role, Pastor Chiweshe continued to excel, leaving a lasting legacy within AFM. His self-awareness and willingness to operate within his sphere of influence demonstrate a vital lesson for ministers: understanding one's divine calling and functioning within the designated role is crucial for maintaining effectiveness and avoiding unnecessary setbacks.

Conversely, individuals called to pioneer and lead independent ministries possess a unique spiritual DNA. For them, the visible church serves as a foundational stepping stone and launchpad, but not a permanent containment. Their visionary leadership and innovative spirit cannot be confined by traditional church structures, as they are driven by an unrelenting passion and divine mandate.

This inner fire, ignited by God's command, burns intensely within them, fueling an insatiable desire to venture beyond the conventional boundaries of church leadership. Like apostolic pioneers, they are compelled to respond to the divine call, even if it means breaking free from the comfort and security of established religious institutions.

As they embark on this journey, they often face challenges and uncertainties, but their unwavering commitment to God's vision propels them forward. Ultimately, they establish new ministries, churches, or movements that reflect their distinctive calling and leadership style, leaving an indelible mark on the spiritual landscape.

In this context, the authentic Apostolic Faith Mission (AFM), founded by the pioneering Apostolic Faith missionaries - Thomas Hezmalhalch, John Graham Lake, and their dedicated team - remains unshakeable, despite experiencing numerous breakaways. These breakaways can be categorized into two types: God-ordained separations, where leaders are divinely called to establish new ministries, and self-motivated departures, driven by personal ambitions or disagreements.

The genuine AFM, rooted in the original vision and principles of its founders, will endure and continue to thrive. Its foundation, built on the solid rock of apostolic teachings and practices, ensures its stability and resilience. Just as a mighty tree withstands seasonal storms and sheds branches, only to grow stronger and more resilient, the authentic AFM will weather the storms of breakaways and emerge more vibrant and purposeful.

The God-ordained breakaways, in particular, will actually contribute to the expansion of the kingdom of God, as they enable the spread of apostolic teachings and the establishment of new ministries, all aligned with the original vision. In this sense, the breakaways become a testament to the AFM's reproductive capacity, demonstrating its ability to multiply and extend its reach, rather than a sign of weakness or decline.

CHAPTER four

Reconciling the Past, Rebuilding the Future

The establishment of Apostolic Faith Mission International (AFMI), headquartered in South Africa, as a unified mother organization for AFM churches across various nations, indicates that the Apostolic Faith Mission of South Africa has relinquished control over AFM churches in other countries. Previously, the South African church had oversight since 1908, until the Zimbabwean mission field demanded autonomy in 1983, which was granted.

Following independence, the AFM in Zimbabwe operated self-sufficiently, planting churches regionally and overseas without requiring permission. These ministries reported directly to the AFM in Zimbabwe, whose members served as missionaries. In response to the growing international presence of AFM Zimbabwe, stakeholders recognized the need for a unified global structure, leading to the formation of AFMI. This development signifies a shift towards a more decentralized and collaborative governance model, acknowledging the autonomy and growth of AFM churches worldwide.

Despite the fact that many prominent overseas Apostolic Faith Mission (AFM) churches are led by presidents from Zimbabwe, these churches are no longer affiliated with AFM in Zimbabwe. Instead, they are now affiliated with Apostolic Faith Mission International (AFMI), to which AFM in Zimbabwe is also an affiliate. In this context, AFM in Zimbabwe, similar to its former parent church, AFM of South Africa, has relinquished jurisdiction over its regional and international offspring churches. These churches now operate under the umbrella of AFMI, marking a significant shift in governance and affiliation.

The breakaways and splits within the Apostolic Faith Mission (AFM) since 1983 had minimal impact on Apostolic Faith Mission International (AFMI) because it was understood that leaving a local AFM church meant severing ties with AFMI. However, the 2018 split had far-reaching consequences for AFMI, which still persist six years later, in 2024.

Unlike previous splits, the 2018 division involved a significant number of high-profile leaders and churches, resulting in a substantial loss of membership, influence, and resources for AFMI. This split exposed underlying issues within AFMI, such as governance, leadership, and affiliation structures, which had not been adequately addressed.

The aftermath of the 2018 split saw a decline in AFMI's global cohesion, as various factions and interests emerged. The organization's reputation was also affected, leading to a loss of credibility and trust among some members and partner organizations.

Despite efforts to address these challenges, AFMI continues to grapple with the consequences of the 2018 split. The ongoing impact is a testament to the complexity and depth of the issues involved, highlighting the need for sustained dialogue, reform, and reconciliation within the organization.

Before we delve deeper into the discussion on Apostolic Faith Mission International (AFMI), let's take a brief detour to examine the complex dynamics that were already affecting AFMI prior to the 2018 split. This detour will provide valuable context and insight into the underlying factors that contributed to the split and its subsequent impact on the organization.

By exploring the pre-2018 landscape, we can gain a better understanding of the intricate web of relationships, power dynamics, and structural issues that existed within AFMI. This will help us appreciate the nuances of the 2018 split and its far-reaching consequences, which still resonate within the organization today.

The Apostolic Faith Mission (AFM) in Zimbabwe, from its inception in 1983 to the 2018 split, experienced a mix of strengths and weaknesses, compounded by various breakaways, some small and others significant. While the church leadership navigated these challenges, they also grappled with internal issues, some of which remained obscure to ordinary members.

Veteran members recall the church had influential, high-contributing members who mysteriously stopped attending services, leaving behind unanswered questions. These individuals had significantly supported the church's projects, including the construction of the Rufaro National

Conference Center near Chatsworth, with substantial financial contributions. Their sudden disappearance fueled speculation and suspicion among members, with some assuming they might have been at odds with political powers or other internal dynamics.

The lack of transparency surrounding these events has led to ongoing speculation and mistrust within the church. Breakaways and splits, therefore, come as no surprise, as they often stem from unseen factors. It's possible that those who break away may have been privy to information that remained hidden from the rest of the congregation.

As the Shona proverb goes, "There is no pool without toads." Both the mother church and breakaway groups have their flaws, reflecting the inherent imperfections of human nature. Rather than assigning blame, it's essential to acknowledge these shortcomings and strive for greater understanding and transparency.

The establishment of Apostolic Faith Mission (AFM) of South Africa's Zimbabwe mission field in 1908 by immigrant workers who received the AFM message in South Africa in May 1908 has a contemporary parallel. Today, immigrant workers in South Africa have formed satellite AFM churches in Zimbabwe, operating under the banner of AFM of South Africa Shona-speaking Assemblies since 2009. These assemblies were recognized by AFM of South Africa as a provision to enable Shona-speakers to access church programs and missions in their native language, thereby extending the South African AFM message to a broader audience.

Although these assemblies were officially part of AFM of South Africa, they functioned as satellite churches of AFM in Zimbabwe. This was made possible by the AFM of South Africa's constitution, which grants local assemblies autonomy to create their own policies and administer the church as they see fit, while reporting to their regional headquarters. This allowed Shona-speaking assemblies to maintain close ties with their counterparts in Zimbabwe, seeking assistance with new pastors, guest speakers, and other needs.

In the case of new pastors for Shona-speaking assemblies, the South African leadership would interview candidates recommended by the local assembly. Pastors seconded to South Africa were considered to be on continuous service in Zimbabwe, without a break in employment. This arrangement enabled individual pastors in leadership positions within AFM in Zimbabwe to receive special cash and kind benefits from Shona-speaking assemblies in South Africa several times a year.

Thus, AFM in Zimbabwe clandestinely operated satellite churches in South Africa, leveraging the autonomy granted by AFM of South Africa's constitution to maintain a presence in the country. This setup allowed for a complex web of relationships between AFM in Zimbabwe and its satellite assemblies in South Africa, with benefits and resources flowing between the two.

For this reason, and in this sense, the 2018 split within the Apostolic Faith Mission (AFM) in Zimbabwe had far-reaching consequences, extending beyond national borders to affect international churches, particularly those with Shona-speaking assemblies in South Africa. Despite the Apostolic Faith Mission International's (AFMI) urgings to contain the conflict, factionalism persisted, fueled by moral and ideological differences rather than physical factors.

In South Africa, Zimbabwean members unite under the AFM of South Africa umbrella, but upon returning home, either permanently or temporarily, they align with either the AFM in Zimbabwe or the AFM of Zimbabwe. This dichotomy is mirrored in overseas churches, where Zimbabweans also divide along the same lines. This phenomenon underscores the existence of factions within the international Zimbabwean church community, albeit subtly.

The attendance patterns of regional and international pastors at national conferences hosted by the two AFMs in Zimbabwe - Rufaro (AFM in Zimbabwe) and Mufaro (AFM of Zimbabwe) - reveal a clear divide. Pastors consistently attend either one or the other, but not both. Similarly, social media groups reflect this split, with members who attend Rufaro conferences joining AFM in Zimbabwe groups, while those who attend Mufaro conferences join

AFM of Zimbabwe groups. This demonstrates the global impact of the 2018 AFM split, particularly within Zimbabwean-led communities worldwide.

The significant presence of Zimbabweans in leadership positions within Apostolic Faith Mission (AFM) International affiliates has created a complex dynamic. With three, four, or more presidents of overseas AFMs hailing from Zimbabwe, and all presidents of AFM International affiliates constituting the Apostolic Faith Mission International (AFMI) board, factionalism following the 2018 split inevitably impacts AFMI's decisions on issues concerning Zimbabwe.

This has resulted in a unique situation where both AFMs operating in Zimbabwe are affiliated with AFMI - the AFM in Zimbabwe as the sole representative per nation, and AFM of Zimbabwe as an associate member. This dual affiliation suggests that AFMI has struggled to effectively address the Zimbabwean church's needs since the 2018 split.

To understand the circumstances surrounding the split, it is essential to examine the events leading up to it, as presented by both sides before AFMI and the courts of law. This includes analyzing the grievances, allegations, and counter-allegations made by the respective factions. Additionally, we will explore the subsequent actions taken by AFMI and the affected parties, including any attempts at reconciliation, mediation, or resolution.

By delving into the intricacies of the 2018 split and its aftermath, we can gain insight into the challenges faced by AFMI in navigating the complex web of relationships within the Zimbabwean church and the global AFM community. This will also shed light on the way forward for AFMI and the Zimbabwean church, as they seek to rebuild and strengthen their relationships in the wake of the split.

The founding of Apostolic Faith Mission International (AFMI) was a significant milestone, but unfortunately, the organization's creators did not anticipate a critical issue that would arise in the future. They did not foresee that citizens of one country could hold presidency positions in multiple countries, and that dual citizenship would not erase their initial citizenship from their hearts.

This phenomenon is not unique to AFMI. For instance, Black people in the United States, despite holding full American citizenship, often identify as African-American, acknowledging their African heritage. This dual identity does not diminish their American rights or privileges. Similarly, when they travel to African countries, they are welcomed as Africans from America.

In the context of AFMI, indigenous Zimbabweans who hold presidency positions in various countries around the world still maintain a strong connection to their Zimbabwean roots. Their hearts remain tied to their homeland, even as they serve in international leadership roles.

The complexity arises when these individuals, now leaders in AFMI, are part of the decision-making body. Their allegiance to their country of origin can sometimes conflict with their responsibilities as AFMI leaders. This has become a challenge, particularly since the former factions in Zimbabwe are now both full members of AFMI.

The issue is not about aligning with either faction back in Zimbabwe, as both are legitimate members of AFMI. However, when it comes to decision-making within AFMI, the loyalty of these leaders to their country of origin can create tensions and conflicts of interest. This highlights the need for AFMI to address this issue and find ways to navigate the complex web of national identities and allegiances within its leadership structure.

In light of this situation, the Apostolic Faith Mission International (AFMI) faces a critical challenge. If left unaddressed, the unresolved factionalism within the Zimbabwean church could potentially spread to the international body, threatening its unity and stability. The AFMI's failure to effectively manage this conflict could lead to the emergence of factions within its own ranks, mirroring the divisions already present in Zimbabwe.

Historically, unchecked factionalism has been a precursor to division and decline in various Christian denominations. If the AFMI does not take proactive measures to address the root causes of this conflict and promote reconciliation, it risks succumbing to the same fate. The consequences would be far-reaching, potentially leading to a decline in membership, influence, and spiritual vitality.

To avoid this outcome, the AFMI must prioritize dialogue, mediation, and conflict resolution. By fostering open communication channels, addressing grievances, and promoting a shared vision, the AFMI can mitigate the risk of factionalism and ensure its continued unity and growth. Only through intentional effort and a commitment to biblical principles of love, forgiveness, and reconciliation can the AFMI safeguard its future and maintain its integrity as a global, Spirit-led movement.

To tackle this pressing issue, the Apostolic Faith Mission International (AFMI) must revisit its foundational principles and re-examine its evolution. Prior to the 1980s, all international mission fields were under the direct control and ownership of the Apostolic Faith Mission of South Africa (AFM-SA), which still exists today. This raises crucial questions: What led to the creation of the AFMI? Who conceived this idea, and what specific challenges did they aim to address? What were the primary concerns that prompted the AFMI to establish affiliate members globally?

A thorough investigation into these questions will help the AFMI understand its historical context and identify potential areas for improvement. Additionally, it is essential to examine the AFMI's constitution, specifically any amendments made since 2018. Which sections were revised, and did these changes address the Zimbabwean situation or other related issues?

By engaging in this introspective process, the AFMI can clarify its purpose and mission, ensuring alignment with its founding principles. It can also identify and rectify any constitutional ambiguities, thereby preventing misinterpretations and potential conflicts. Furthermore, this self-examination enables the AFMI to strengthen its relationship with affiliate members, fostering trust and cooperation. Through this process, the AFMI can develop effective strategies to mitigate factionalism, addressing the root causes of division and promoting unity. Ultimately, this introspection can enhance the AFMI's global unity and cohesion, allowing it to move forward with renewed purpose and strength.

Only through this deliberate and transparent self-examination can the AFMI hope to resolve its internal conflicts, address the Zimbabwean issue, and ensure its continued relevance and effectiveness as a global, Spirit-led movement.

Prior to the court's declaratory judgment and other reliefs, both factions claimed to be the authentic Apostolic Faith Mission (AFM) in Zimbabwe. Therefore, when referring to AFM in Zimbabwe before the judgment, we are essentially talking about a unified church that existed before the split.

Following the split, the original church retained the name "AFM in Zimbabwe," while the breakaway faction adopted the name "AFM of Zimbabwe." This new entity distinguished itself with a modified version of the original logo, featuring different colors. This rebranding effort underscored the breakaway church's desire to establish a distinct identity, separate from the original AFM in Zimbabwe.

In essence, the court's judgment helped clarify the identities of the two factions, confirming AFM in Zimbabwe as the original church and AFM of Zimbabwe as the breakaway church. This distinction is important for understanding the history and development of the two entities, particularly in the context of their affiliation with Apostolic Faith Mission International (AFMI).

When recounting historical events, it's essential to rely on verifiable evidence and actual occurrences rather than solely on the claims of one faction. In the case of the Apostolic Faith Mission (AFM) split, AFM of Zimbabwe, led by Rev. C. Chiangwa, continues to assert that it is the original church that existed before the split. However, tangible evidence contradicts this claim.

The legal battle between the two factions of the Apostolic Faith Mission in Zimbabwe began on October 4, 2018, when the then-sitting president filed a court case (HC 9149/18) in the High Court of Harare. However, it wasn't until January 10, 2019, that the then-deputy president, Rev. C. Chiangwa, and others filed their own case (HC 179/19). The delay in filing their case raises questions about their strategy and preparedness.

Notably, both factions claimed to have the authority to sue and be sued as the legitimate AFM in Zimbabwe, which led the astute judge to consolidate the two cases. This consolidation resulted in a single judgment being delivered on September 4, 2019, for the combined case ([2019] ZWHHC 586). The court ruled in favor of the initial case ("[2019] ZWHHC 9149), while dismissing the second case ([2019] ZWHHC 179) with costs. This outcome had significant implications for the leadership and legitimacy of the Apostolic Faith Mission in Zimbabwe.

Undeterred by the High Court's decision, the losing party, led by Rev. C. Chiangwa, appealed to the Supreme Court, seeking to overturn the ruling. However, on May 28, 2021, the Supreme Court delivered its verdict (Judgment No. SC 67/21), dismissing the appeal in its entirety. Furthermore, the court ordered the losing party to bear the costs of the appeal, solidifying the original judgment and reaffirming the legitimacy of the opposing faction as the authentic Apostolic Faith Mission in Zimbabwe. This definitive ruling brought closure to the protracted legal battle, underscoring the finality of the courts' decisions.

The Chiangwa faction then introduced a new logo, adopted a distinct name, AFM of Zimbabwe, and established new venues for their assembly gatherings and conferences. These changes suggest that they are, in fact, the breakaway faction.

The other faction, declared as AFM in Zimbabwe, has maintained continuity with the pre-split church by retaining all the original elements. They have kept the same logo and branding, continued to use the same venues for their gatherings and conferences that were used before the split, and implemented an amended draft constitution that was initiated before the split. Furthermore, the primary cause of the split, as documented in court papers, was the controversial constitution amendment project, which was a point of contention between the two factions. By retaining these original elements, AFM in Zimbabwe has demonstrated its commitment to preserving the identity and heritage of the pre-split church.

These facts indicate that AFM in Zimbabwe has maintained continuity with the pre-split church, while AFM of Zimbabwe has introduced significant changes, underscoring its status as the breakaway faction. By examining the evidence and actual events, we can reconstruct an accurate historical account of the AFM split.

To ensure a fair and impartial examination of the events surrounding the Apostolic Faith Mission (AFM) split, we will carefully consider the court presentation made by the losing party, AFM of Zimbabwe led by Rev. C. Chiangwa. We assume that their testimony was given under oath, and therefore, we have no reason to doubt the sincerity of their statements. Similarly, we will take the declarations made by church leaders at face value, assuming they genuinely believed in the claims they made.

By analyzing the losing party's court presentation and the statements of church leaders, we aim to assess the validity of their claim to being the original AFM in Zimbabwe (1983 to present). This approach will enable us to evaluate the evidence presented and determine whether their claim holds merit or is lacking in substance. Through this examination, we hope to gain a deeper understanding of the events that led to the split and the legitimacy of each faction's claims.

CHAPTER five

The Anatomy of a Church Split

As previously noted, our focus on the party that ultimately lost in court, after years of protracted litigation, offers valuable insights into the strategies and missteps that can lead to defeat in a prolonged legal battle. While it may seem that we are devoting more attention to the losing side, our intention is not to disparage or criticize, but rather to dissect and analyze the factors that contributed to their loss. By doing so, we aim to uncover the techniques and tactics that can make or break a case, and how consistency and perseverance can ultimately lead to triumph.

It is essential to acknowledge that both factions had unwavering faith and hope in the same God, yet their differing interpretations and approaches led to a bitter split. Our examination of the losing side is not intended to be harsh or judgmental, but rather to provide a nuanced understanding of the events that unfolded. By exploring the why and how behind their loss, we can gain a deeper appreciation for the importance of steadfastness and the dangers of vacillating in one's stance.

Through this in-depth analysis, we hope to distill valuable lessons about the importance of consistency, strategic planning, and effective communication. We will also examine the winning side's strategies and tactics, highlighting the factors that contributed to their success. By exploring both sides of the conflict, we aim to gain a comprehensive understanding of the complex issues that led to the split and the legitimacy of each faction's claims. Ultimately, our goal is to provide a balanced and insightful account of this pivotal event in the history of the Apostolic Faith Mission in Zimbabwe.

Now, as we venture further into this complex case, let us meticulously dissect the delicate interplay between truth, evidence, and righteousness. Through this in-depth examination, we may unearth profound insights into the human condition, laying bare the vital importance of discernment, critical thinking, and the unwavering pursuit of justice.

By peeling back the layers of this multifaceted issue, we will gain a deeper understanding of the intricate relationships between facts, perceptions, and moral principles. This nuanced exploration will illuminate the essential role of critical thinking in navigating the gray areas between truth and deception, and the paramount importance of discernment in distinguishing right from wrong.

Ultimately, our inquiry will reveal the transformative power of justice, highlighting its capacity to redeem and restore individuals, communities, and institutions. Through this thoughtful analysis, we will distill valuable lessons about the human experience, underscoring the need for vigilance, critical inquiry, and an unwavering commitment to truth and righteousness.

In addition to examining the validity of each faction's claims, we will also assess whether any technical issues raised are capable of resolving the dispute or are simply irrelevant and immaterial. The courts' primary role is to resolve conflicts in a fair and efficient manner, providing a just outcome for all parties involved.

Introducing irrelevant technicalities can only serve to waste valuable time and hinder the progress of the case, without offering any benefits to either party. Such exercises in futility can lead to unnecessary delays, increased costs, and a lack of clarity, ultimately undermining the effectiveness of the legal process.

Therefore, it is essential to focus on the core issues at hand and avoid raising frivolous technical points that do not contribute to the resolution of the dispute. By doing so, the courts can ensure that their decisions are based on the merits of the case, rather than being sidetracked by irrelevant technicalities.

From the outset, it was evident that one faction would ultimately lose the court battle. The fact that both Madziyire and Chiangwa relied on the same constitution, which was identical in all essential aspects, meant that the dispute would hinge on the interpretation and application of the same set of rules. Since both factions accused each other of violating the constitution and church regulations, the court's decision would necessarily depend on a meticulous examination of these governing documents. In essence, the courts would have to uphold or nullify the actions of either faction based on their adherence to the church's constitution and regulations. This meant that the faction whose arguments were less aligned with the constitution and regulations would inevitably face defeat, making the outcome of the court battle somewhat predictable from the start.

Our objective goes beyond merely recounting the events leading to the split; we aim to scrutinize the actions of believer leaders within the believers' church through the lens of faith. As they present their cases and defend their causes before civil courts, do they recall the scripture's promise that "the truth shall set you free" (John 8:32)? Do they remember the commandment to "not bear false witness against your neighbor" (Exodus 20:16)?

Church leaders must recognize that their actions are under divine scrutiny, as Proverbs 5:21 states, "The ways of man are before the eyes of the LORD, and he ponders all man's goings." As they address their congregants, the public, and the courts, are they aware that God's eyes are upon them, observing all their actions (Proverbs 15:3)?

In their endeavors, do they acknowledge that if their deeds are not done for the Lord's glory, He will expose their true intentions (1 Corinthians 4:5)? Our goal is to caution the audience against toying with fire, for the Lord is a consuming fire (Hebrews 12:29). We urge them to heed the warning in 1 Corinthians 3:13, "Each man's work will become manifest; for the Day will disclose it, because it will be revealed with fire, and the fire will test what sort of work each one has done."

By examining the actions of church leaders through a biblical lens, we hope to encourage the audience to prioritize truth, integrity, and accountability, recognizing that their actions have eternal consequences.

Our narrative will unfold chronologically, meticulously tracing the key events, milestones, and turning points that ultimately led to the split and formation of the Apostolic Faith Mission of Zimbabwe (AFM of Zimbabwe), a distinct entity from the Apostolic Faith Mission in Zimbabwe (AFM in Zimbabwe). As we navigate this complex journey, we will pause to thoroughly examine significant themes and issues that arise, exploring their far-reaching implications and impact on the church. This in-depth analysis will enable us to grasp the intricacies and nuances of the events leading up to the official split.

Throughout our narrative, we will also highlight the critical intersections and relationships with the Apostolic Faith Mission International (AFMI), the mother board or council that oversees all national AFM churches globally. Understanding these connections is crucial, as they played a pivotal role in shaping the course of events and influencing the ultimate outcome.

By adopting this approach, we will gain a comprehensive understanding of the complex factors that contributed to the split, as well as the official formation of the AFM of Zimbabwe as a distinct entity. Our chronological narrative will be interspersed with in-depth analyses, providing a rich and detailed account of the journey that led to this significant development in the history of the Apostolic Faith Mission.

For clarity and convenience, the two rival factions in the Apostolic Faith Mission (AFM) in Zimbabwe will be referred to by interchangeable names. The faction led by President Dr. Aspher Madziyire can be referred to as the reform side, reformist side, pro-reformists, Madawo faction, or simply Madziyire or Madawo. This faction has been synonymous with the AFM in Zimbabwe since Rev Madziyire assumed office as president.

On the other hand, the faction led by Deputy President Rev Cossum Chiangwa can be referred to as the anti-reformist side, anti-reform side, or simply Chiangwa. Following the Supreme Court judgment, this faction has also been referred to as the AFM of Zimbabwe or Apostolic Faith Mission of Zimbabwe.

It is essential to note that the AFM in Zimbabwe refers to the church as a whole, but when used in the context of the conflict, it typically denotes the Madziyire faction, which has been the status quo since Rev Madziyire's presidency. The Chiangwa faction, on the other hand, emerged as a distinct entity after the Supreme Court ruling, which led to a split within the church.

14 April 2015

According to a NewsDay report on April 14, 2015, a fierce leadership wrangle rocked the Apostolic Faith Mission (AFM) in Zimbabwe, raising fears that the Pentecostal church could be heading for a split. The controversy centered on the church's presidential and overseers' elections, which some pastors and elders claimed were conducted unconstitutionally.

As reported by Phyllis Mbanje, the disgruntled clergymen took their administrators to court, seeking to nullify Reverend Aspher Madziyire's election as president. According to court documents, the plaintiffs alleged that Madziyire created three new provinces - Manicaland East, Murewa, and Mashonaland Central - to sway the election results in his favor. They also claimed that he was elected without the consent of the church's workers' council, which was supposed to form an electoral college to vote for the president.

The report stated that the disgruntled clergymen, represented by lawyer Zivanai Macharaga, gave Madziyire and the church's leadership 10 days to respond to their allegations.

Bishop Christopher Choto, secretary of the church's national leadership forum, addressed a press conference, stating that the bone of contention was the unconstitutional presidential elections. He emphasized that the concerns of congregants and the victimization of pastors had driven them to seek legal action.

It is evident that the Pastors Fraternity, a collective of pastors within the Apostolic Faith Mission (AFM) in Zimbabwe, has a rich history that stretches back beyond 2015. This suggests that the group has a established presence and a long-standing role within the AFM in Zimbabwe, with roots that extend further than the 2015 timeline. The fraternity's history is likely marked by significant events, milestones, and contributions to the church, shaping its identity and influence within the AFM community. However, it was after the 2015 elections that their grievances came to the forefront. Bishop Christopher Choto, then secretary of the church's national leadership forum, revealed that their 2015 court challenge stemmed from allegations of unconstitutional presidential elections. Ironically, the national leadership forum itself was operating unconstitutionally.

Choto highlighted the concerns of congregants who were dissatisfied with the election process, leading to victimization and intimidation of pastors. This resulted in widespread divisions within the church. It appears that the rift had been growing over the years, fueled by sour grapes from pastors who lost in the 2015 elections. Rev Madziyire, who had served multiple terms in office, seemed to have accumulated more enemies than allies.

The Pastors Fraternity sought to address constitutional concerns but ended up violating the same principles. Their actions suggest a desire for power and control, rather than a genuine pursuit of constitutional integrity. This paradox raises questions about their true motives and the legitimacy of their claims.

The situation exposes a deeper issue within the AFM, where leadership struggles and power dynamics have created divisions and conflicts. The church's inability to address these concerns internally has led to external interventions, including court battles, further exacerbating the crisis.

The Pastors Fraternity, also known as the Pastors Forum, is a shadowy group within the Apostolic Faith Mission (AFM) in Zimbabwe that operates like a clandestine workers council, bypassing constitutional channels to further their agenda. Just as workers in the secular world have workers' committees to address grievances, these pastors have created a parallel forum, not sanctioned by the church's constitution, to pursue their interests. This unofficial "workers council" has become a powerful force, driving divisions and conflicts within the church. Like a clandestine union, they wield significant influence, often using their collective power to challenge the official leadership. However, their actions raise questions about their true motives and the legitimacy of their claims, exposing a deeper crisis of leadership and power dynamics within the AFM.

The Apostolic Faith Mission (AFM) in Zimbabwe operated without a formal dispute resolution process, relying on an informal tradition of censuring offenders without a written procedure. This lack of a clear process created a vacuum, leaving pastors with no official channel to address their grievances, including work-related and salary issues. In response, the Pastors Fraternity emerged as a pressure group, seeking to fill this gap and advocate for change.

Although the Pastors Fraternity or forum may seem like an opposing force, it's not quite accurate to label it as such at this point. Initially, the group represented a collective voice for reform and stood for various principles, rather than being a direct opposition to the existing leadership or structures. The Constitutional Reforms themselves had not yet become a contentious issue.

Furthermore, the church's policy documents, intended to support pastors, became a source of contention. For instance, the policy providing for school fees assistance (up to 50% tuition and levy for public schools) and rural allowances (15% of basic salary) created disparities and disputes. With some assemblies struggling to pay their pastors' salaries, let alone the additional allowances, tensions arose between urban and rural pastors.

The real crux of the dispute lay in the unequal distribution of resources, with urban pastors resisting the centralization of funds to ensure equal pay for their rural counterparts. Led by urban pastors, the Pastors Fraternity opposed constitutional amendments, fearing a loss of power and control. The situation escalated in 2015 and reached a boiling point in 2018, exposing deep-seated issues within the AFM.

The absence of a formal dispute resolution process and the lack of transparency in resource allocation fueled the conflict, highlighting the need for a more equitable and structured approach to addressing grievances and allocating resources within the church.

Given the existence of these and other constitutional loopholes, a comprehensive review of the church's constitution, regulations, and policies was necessary. To better understand the current conflict surrounding the reforms, let's take a moment to examine the background of the Constitutional Review Process (CRP), and the initial catalysts that sparked the controversy.

In 2009, newly appointed Secretary General Overseer Madawo, elected by the Workers Council, discovered minutes from previous meetings highlighting the need to amend the constitution. Legal advisors had warned that the growing membership had outpaced the provisions of the constitution, leading to a dilution of spiritual values.

In response, the 2015 Workers Council resolved to amend the constitution, with a focus on addressing several critical issues, including the lack of accountability, inadequate transparency, insufficient checks and balances, and inequitable financial management. These issues had been identified as major concerns that needed to be addressed in order to ensure the church's governance structure was robust and effective.

A Constitution Review Committee (CRC) was formed in 2015, comprising experts from various fields, including law, human resources, and accounting. They worked together to create a draft constitution, which was intended to be reviewed by the Apostolic Council, then sent to provinces for input, and finally returned to the Workers Council.

However, the draft was leaked to the public, causing widespread disturbance among congregants. Despite this setback, the Apostolic Council received the draft from the provinces at the end of 2017 and accepted it, acknowledging that it was incomplete but necessary for progress. The plan was to refine it further during the 2018 triennial elections.

Unfortunately, some pastors from the forum, fearing their own interests would be compromised, began spreading false claims and propaganda against the leadership. This created a toxic atmosphere, leading to chaos and conflict in 2018. The events from 2018 onwards will be discussed in detail, later, covering a period of six years, until 2024.

Now, back to our story. Before delving into the chronological events, it's essential to highlight that many of the financial provisions in the amended Apostolic Faith Mission (AFM) in Zimbabwe's draft constitution, which sparked controversy and ultimately led to the split, mirror those in the Constitution of Zimbabwe. Rejecting these provisions would be equivalent to rejecting the country's chief law. Let's examine a specific example.

The amended AFM constitution establishes a Consolidated Revenue Fund, which reads:

37.1 A Consolidated Revenue Fund is hereby established into which must be paid all tithes, offerings, collections, levies, gifts, fees, borrowings, and all other revenues of the Church, whatever their source, unless an Act of the General National Council:

37.1.1 Requires or permits them to be paid into some other fund established for a specific purpose; or

37.1.2 Permits the recipient to retain them, or part of them, in order to meet expenses approved by the General National Council.

Similarly, the Constitution of Zimbabwe (Chapter 17, FINANCE) establishes a Consolidated Revenue Fund, stating:

1. Consolidated Revenue Fund

There is a Consolidated Revenue Fund into which must be paid all fees, taxes, and borrowings and all other revenues of the Government, whatever their source, unless an Act of Parliament:

a. requires or permits them to be paid into some other fund established for a specific purpose; or

b. permits the authority that received them to retain them, or part of them, in order to meet the authority's expenses.

The striking similarity between these two provisions underscores the notion that the amended AFM constitution's financial provisions are not revolutionary or unusual but rather align with the country's existing legal framework. This raises questions about the motivations behind the opposition to these provisions and the subsequent split within the AFM.

Let's now revisit the sequence of events that led to the eventual split, tracing back to the beginning of 2018 - a year that will forever be etched in the memory of the Apostolic Faith Mission (AFM) of Zimbabwe as the turning point when the seeds of division were sown. This pivotal year marked the starting point of a chain of events that would ultimately lead to the fragmentation of the church. By examining the chronology of events, we can gain a deeper understanding of the circumstances that contributed to the split and how the situation unfolded over time.

CHAPTER six

The Struggle for Leadership and Governance

On February 3, 2018, the Apostolic Council convened at Rufaro Conference Centre, where they made a significant decision: to proceed with elections under the current constitution, while postponing constitutional reforms until after the elections. This resolution was in line with the standard protocol, which required the Apostolic Council to present their decisions to the Workers Council, the highest decision-making body in the Apostolic Faith Mission in Zimbabwe, for endorsement, rejection, or amendment.

The Workers Council, scheduled to meet on February 10, 2018, held the final authority to shape the course of action. Their deliberations would determine whether to:

1. Endorse the Apostolic Council's resolution, paving the way for elections under the current constitution.

2. Reject the resolution, potentially halting the election process.

3. Amend the resolution, introducing changes to the proposed plan.

This critical meeting would have far-reaching implications for the Apostolic Faith Mission in Zimbabwe, influencing the trajectory of the organization's leadership, governance, and future direction.

The Apostolic Council, a high-level decision-making body, was composed of mostly Overseers, the President, Secretary General, and the Principal of Living Waters Theological Seminary, and heads of ministries such as the Welfare, who were all pastors, with one or two lay workers against about thirty-five pastors. However, the Workers Council, the highest decision-making authority, had a different composition, with a ratio of one pastor to six lay workers, giving lay workers a substantial voice in decision-making. This meant that the Workers Council held considerable power to shape the organization's direction, and if the lay workers, who formed the majority, disagreed with the Apostolic

Council's resolutions, they could easily reject them, outweighing the pastors' votes.

An entrenched, unconstitutional tradition had taken hold within the Apostolic Faith Mission in Zimbabwe, perpetuated by pastors at every level, from assembly to national. At the assembly level, pastors would often co-opt influential congregants, rendering lay workers powerless and ensuring that the majority sided with the pastor, even when they erred. This created a culture of impunity, where pastors were rarely held accountable for their actions.

At the provincial level, Overseers would exploit this dynamic, courting disgruntled lay workers from assemblies and leveraging their support to maintain power. When elections for new Overseers were held, the incumbent would typically prevail, thanks to the backing of lay workers who felt valued and supported by the Overseer.

This tradition continued unabated at the national level, where the sitting president would consistently win re-election. However, both Overseers and pastors would cry foul at the provincial and national levels, respectively, bemoaning the very corruption they had instigated at the assembly level. The Constitution Review Process aimed to address this deeply ingrained tradition, which had undermined the organization's democratic processes and created a culture of entitlement among pastors and Overseers.

10 February 2018

From August 2015, the Apostolic Faith Mission in Zimbabwe embarked on a comprehensive constitutional review process (CRP). Led by the Apostolic Council and Workers Council, the initiative was overseen by a Constitutional Review Committee (CRC), chaired by Elder T Nyambirai. The committee's objective was to address critical issues in electoral processes, financial management, and governance through constitutional amendments. The ultimate goals were to guarantee free, fair, and credible church elections, foster accountability and transparency, and ensure equal opportunities and fair treatment for clergy and church development programs across all regions.

The CRP culminated in the Extraordinary General Meeting of the Workers Council on February 10, 2018, which resolved to hold the triennial Provincial and Workers Council elections on April 28, 2018. This was contingent upon the Workers Council considering and approving the proposed constitutional amendments at its scheduled meeting on April 28, 2018. The CRP was a comprehensive review of the church's constitution, ensuring it remained relevant and effective in governing the organization.

It is crucial to note that the meeting held on February 10, 2018, was an Extraordinary General Meeting of the Workers Council, marking the culmination of the CRP. This process was spearheaded by the CRC. The CRP was a comprehensive review of the church's constitution, aimed at ensuring it remained relevant and effective in governing the organization.

The meeting proposed for February 18, 2018, played a significant role in shaping the CRP, as it laid the groundwork for the subsequent discussions and decisions made during the Extraordinary General Meeting. The CRC, under Elder Nyambirai's leadership, worked tirelessly to facilitate a thorough review of the constitution, soliciting input from various stakeholders and incorporating their suggestions into the revised document.

The Constitutional Review Process (CRP) spanned several significant events, including the initiation of the process in August 2015.

A detailed examination of the resolutions made by the Apostolic Council and the Workers Council meetings reveals a significant development. The Workers Council effectively rejected the Apostolic Council's resolution, opting to modify it instead. On February 3, 2018, the Apostolic Council had made a crucial decision: to proceed with elections under the current constitution, while postponing constitutional reforms until after the elections. However, the Workers Council, in its Extraordinary General Meeting on February 10, 2018, resolved to hold the triennial Provincial and Workers Council elections on April 28, 2018, but with a critical condition.

The Workers Council stipulated that the elections would only proceed if they considered and approved the proposed constitutional amendments at their scheduled meeting on April 28, 2018. This move marked a significant departure from the Apostolic Council's original resolution, demonstrating the Workers Council's assertion of its authority and its commitment to addressing the long-standing need for constitutional reforms. By making the elections contingent upon the approval of the constitutional amendments, the Workers Council ensured that the organization's leadership and governance structure would be reformed before the next cycle of elections, paving the way for a more democratic and representative Apostolic Faith Mission in Zimbabwe.

This leads us to the deep-seated issues stemming from an entrenched, unconstitutional tradition that had taken root within the church, perpetuated by pastors at all levels, from local assemblies to the national leadership. At the assembly level, pastors would frequently co-opt influential congregants, marginalizing lay workers and ensuring that the majority sided with the pastor, even when they made mistakes. This created a culture of blind loyalty, where congregants prioritized supporting their pastor over holding them accountable.

As this tradition evolved and moved up the hierarchical ladder, it manifested at the national level, where the majority of elders typically favored the president and his team. This resulted in a power imbalance, where the leadership's interests were prioritized over the needs and concerns of the general membership. The entrenched tradition of favoritism and loyalty over accountability enabled leaders to act with impunity, further exacerbating the problems within the church.

This toxic dynamic was perpetuated by a lack of transparency, inadequate checks and balances, and a general disregard for the church's constitution. The consequences were far-reaching, leading to widespread disillusionment, mistrust, and ultimately, the erosion of the church's foundation. The failure to address these issues and adhere to constitutional governance principles paved the way for the conflicts and divisions that would eventually split the church.

The issue will persist, with elders appearing to be at odds with pastors, when in reality, it is the consequences of pastors' mistreatment of lay workers, including elders, at the assembly level that Overseers and the President exploit. The root of the problem lies in the pastors' failure to collaborate with elders at the assembly level, leading to a lack of support and trust from the elders. This, in turn, hinders pastors' ability to succeed in provincial and national councils.

The CRP's intended introduction of a non-executive chairman from the assembly level to the national level was aiming to address this issue by providing checks and balances. This move aimed to encourage pastors to work collaboratively with elders at the assembly level, ensuring that elders' voices are heard and valued, preventing the exploitation of lay workers by pastors and higher-level leaders, and fostering a more democratic and inclusive decision-making process. By implementing this structural change, the organization sought to break the cycle of mistrust and power struggles, promoting a more harmonious and effective leadership dynamic.

By implementing this structural change, the organization sought to break the cycle of mistrust and power struggles, promoting a more harmonious and effective leadership dynamic.

Rev Madziyire was first elected to office in 2003 and went on to serve an unprecedented five terms, winning each subsequent election. At the time, there was no established limit on the number of terms an individual could serve, allowing Rev Madziyire to continue in office for an extended period. His remarkable tenure was marked by consecutive electoral victories, with no legal restrictions in place to limit the number of his three-year terms in office. This lack of term limits enabled Rev Madziyire to maintain his position for a record-breaking five terms, shaping the organization's leadership landscape during his extended tenure.

In the absence of regulatory laws, a president could potentially serve for life, accumulating immense power and influence. The Apostolic Faith Mission of South Africa's history illustrates this, with its early leaders setting important precedents. Thomas Hezmalhalch, the first president, laid the foundation for the organization, followed by John Graham Lake, who expanded its reach. P E LeRoux, the third president, demonstrated remarkable leadership, voluntarily stepping down in 1943 after an impressive thirty years of service, citing old age. This selfless act contrasts with Rev Dr Madziyire's tenure, who served for fifteen years, half the duration of Rev LeRoux's presidency.

Rev LeRoux's thirty-year presidency was marked by significant milestones, including the registration of the church in Zimbabwe by Enoch Gwanzura in 1943, the year LeRoux retired. The fact that Rev LeRoux served for thirty years without facing opposition or term limits highlights the importance of leadership succession and regulatory frameworks in preventing the concentration of power. In contrast, Rev Dr Madziyire's fifteen-year tenure, although significant, pales in comparison to Rev LeRoux's remarkable three-decade leadership.

One of the key objectives of the Constitutional Review Process was to establish a regulatory framework that would prevent the concentration of power and promote democratic leadership by limiting the length of time an individual can hold office. This proposed law aimed to introduce term limits, ensuring that leaders would serve for a defined period, rather than potentially holding power for life. By doing so, the Apostolic Faith Mission in Zimbabwe sought to prevent the negative consequences of prolonged leadership, such as abuse of power, stagnation, and the suppression of new ideas and perspectives. The introduction of term limits would promote accountability, transparency, and the rotation of leadership, ultimately strengthening the church's democratic foundations.

18 February 2018

Following the Extraordinary General Meeting of the Workers Council on February 10, 2018, another meeting was convened on February 18, 2018, to contribute to the CRP's progress. As scheduled meeting on April 28, 2018, was set to consider constitutional amendments and hold elections.

On February 18, 2018, both hard and soft copies of the draft constitution and amendment documents were distributed to all relevant structures within the Apostolic Faith Mission in Zimbabwe. This dissemination of documents was done in preparation for the scheduled Workers Council meeting on April 28, 2018.

During this meeting, the council members were tasked with reviewing the draft documents, debating their content, and potentially proposing amendments. If the council deemed the documents fit, they would then proceed to pass the proposed amendments to the Constitution of the Apostolic Faith Mission in Zimbabwe, either in their original form or with modifications. This process was designed to ensure that all stakeholders had a chance to contribute to the revision of the constitution, fostering a sense of ownership and inclusivity within the organization. The distribution of documents to all structures demonstrates a commitment to transparency and accountability, allowing for a thorough examination of the proposed changes before any decisions were made.

The February 18, 2018, meeting played a significant role in shaping the CRP, laying the groundwork for subsequent discussions and decisions made during the Extraordinary General Meeting. The CRC solicited input from various stakeholders, incorporating their suggestions into the revised document. By involving stakeholders in the review process, the church ensured the revised constitution reflected the collective wisdom and values of its members, ultimately strengthening its governance structure.

CHAPTER seven

The Root Causes of the Chain of Flaws

Rev Chiangwa issued a notice on March 13, 2018, convening a meeting at AFM's Rufaro Mission for that weekend. This was in response to a demand letter or pre-litigation letter from Wasara and Associates. Contrary to a court order, this letter aimed to resolve the dispute amicably, avoiding litigation and saving time, costs, and resources for all parties involved. However, Rev. Chiangwa overlooked the potential consequences of adhering to demands that contravene the constitution, prioritizing expediency over constitutional integrity.

By acting on the demand letter, Rev. Chiangwa may have inadvertently undermined the rule of law and the constitutional framework governing the church. This decision may have far-reaching implications, potentially creating a precedent for future disputes and compromising the stability of the institution.

14 March 2018

Following the call for a Workers Council meeting by Deputy President Rev C Chiangwa, President Dr. A. Madziyire swiftly declared the meeting illegitimate through a letter dated March 14, 2018, written by Rev Madawo, the Secretary General. In the letter, Rev Madawo cited the Regulations, stating that only the President has the authority to preside over the Apostolic Council and Workers Council, and is responsible for overseeing Overseers and Pastors. Therefore, Rev Chiangwa's notice calling for a Workers Council meeting on March 17, 2018, was deemed unlawful and an attempt to assume the President's mandate.

Moreover, the official Workers Council meeting was already scheduled for April 28, 2018, making Rev Chiangwa's actions appear to be a deliberate attempt to undermine the President's authority. The Deputy President's actions were perceived as insubordination and contempt of the Workers Council, further exacerbating the power struggle within the organization.

This move by President Madziyire and Rev Madawo highlighted the deepening divisions within the leadership and the increasing tensions between the President and the Deputy President. The dispute centered on the interpretation of the Regulations and the limits of authority, with each side accusing the other of overstepping their bounds. The situation would continue to escalate, ultimately contributing to the split within the Apostolic Faith Mission.

18 March 2018

A report in the Sunday Mail on March 18, 2018, stated that a power struggle within the Apostolic Faith Mission (AFM) in Zimbabwe threatened to split the church, as top officials engaged in counter-plots to oust each other.

President Dr. Aspher Madziyire and his allies were at odds with Deputy President Rev Cossum Chiangwa, with tensions escalating to secretly recorded conversations and leaked audio recordings.

A group of disgruntled pastors had written to Rev Chiangwa, calling for a motion of no confidence in Dr. Madziyire, who had led the church for over 15 years. However, Dr. Madziyire's faction had declared the meeting illegal, citing constitutional provisions.

Leaked audio recordings revealed top officials' clandestine efforts to gain the upper hand, including Dr. Madziyire's strategy to manipulate the constitutional amendment process and Rev. Madawo's admission to falsifying Dr. Madziyire's signature on a letter. The recordings exposed deep-seated divisions and mistrust within the church's highest echelons.

The power struggle centered on constitutional reforms, with critics arguing that the changes aimed to extend Dr. Madziyire's tenure and pave the way for Rev. Madawo's succession.

Over 650 pastors, 16 overseers, and numerous lay workers had called for a halt to the divisive reforms and to proceed with elections as planned.

Upon examining this press report, it's clear that the actions of both factions fall short of expectations. Neither faction has demonstrated exemplary conduct, and their actions have likely caused harm to the church's reputation and relationships. Both factions have exposed their weaknesses and strengths.

Dr. Aspher Madziyire's faction has demonstrated a strong grip on power, with a deep understanding of constitutional provisions to declare the meeting illegal. However, their tactics have been marred by clandestine efforts, including manipulating the constitutional amendment process and falsifying signatures, revealing a willingness to bend rules to maintain control. Although the forgery of the signature may have been intended to expedite the process for the benefit of the church, the fact remains that forgery is still a serious offense, regardless of the motivations behind it. The ends do not justify the means, and the integrity of the church demands transparency and honesty in all its dealings. Forgery, no matter how well-intentioned, undermines trust and credibility, and cannot be justified as a means to achieve a desired outcome.

On the other hand, Rev Cossum Chiangwa's faction has shown strength in mobilizing support, with over 650 pastors, 16 overseers, and numerous lay workers calling for a halt to the reforms and proceeding with elections. Their ability to secretly record conversations and leak audio recordings has also brought attention to the faction's concerns. However, secretly recording a phone conversation without the other person's consent, with the intention of undermining them, is a serious criminal offense. Just as Rev Madawo's forgery is unacceptable, so too is the illicit recording of private conversations. Both actions violate ethical standards and legal boundaries, and can have severe consequences. Such behavior erodes trust, undermines relationships, and can lead to legal repercussions.

The Chiangwa faction's decision to call for a motion of no confidence in Dr. Madziyire may be seen as a weakness, as it could be perceived as a personal attack rather than a genuine concern for the church's well-being.

Ultimately, the power struggle highlights the need for transparency, accountability, and democratic leadership within the church. The leaked recordings and clandestine efforts have eroded trust among top officials, and the church's highest echelons are now divided. A peaceful resolution that prioritizes the church's interests over individual ambitions is crucial to prevent a split and maintain the integrity of the AFM.

One commentator astutely observed that in the phone call recordings, the Chiangwa faction cleverly deceived the Madziyire faction into believing they shared a common goal. The fact that someone would confess to forgery, under the guise of expediting a process, reveals a deep level of trust. However, this trust was exploited, exposing the perpetrator as duplicitous and manipulative - a "snake in the grass" who preyed on the trust of others. Furthermore, this actions also resemble those of a "witch hunter", seeking to discredit and undermine others for personal gain.

25 March 2018

On March 25, 2018, The Sunday Mail's Religious Affairs Acting Editor reported that the Apostolic Faith Mission in Zimbabwe (AFM) president, Dr. Aspher Madziyire, had been granted a temporary reprieve from facing elections to choose his successor, thanks to the intervention of international leader, Professor Frank Chikane.

Prof. Chikane, from AFM headquarters in South Africa, visited Zimbabwe to address the church's leadership crisis and held meetings with the AFM in Zimbabwe leadership at Living Waters Theological College in Harare. The goal was to resolve the long-standing power struggle between Dr. Madziyire and his deputy, Reverend Cossum Chiangwa.

Dr. Madziyire's faction had previously postponed elections scheduled for January, while a group of pastors petitioned Rev. Chiangwa to demand the polls. Dr. Madziyire sought to introduce constitutional reforms that would extend his 15-year presidency and ensure his preferred successor takes over. Following the meetings, it was decided to postpone elections until the church's constitutional reform process was complete.

A joint letter signed by Pastor Madawo and Dr. Madziyire outlined the resolutions, including the cancellation of the April 14, 2018, workers council meeting and the resumption of the constitution reforms process. The proposed reforms aim to introduce a new grading system for pastors, equalize salaries, and transfer day-to-day church management responsibilities from pastors to elders and deacons.

However, a leaked audio recording revealed that Dr. Madziyire intends to selectively manipulate the constitutional amendments to maintain control and influence, using overseers and pastors to push for certain changes while rejecting others.

Upon examining this press report, it's clear that some information has not been verified. The press has largely relied on information from the Chiangwa faction, which has sometimes provided false or misleading accounts of the Madziyire faction's actions. This has created a skewed narrative, with the Chiangwa faction appearing more transparent and the Madziyire faction seeming more secretive.

The draft constitution proposed by the Madziyire faction has been misinterpreted, with some claiming it aimed to extend his presidency and secure his preferred successor. However, there was never a proposal or provision for the president to choose a successor, as all leadership positions are filled through elections. In fact, the Apostolic Faith Mission in Zimbabwe has never had a succession plan since its inception as the Apostolic Faith Mission of South Africa in 1908. The church was established on May 25, 1908, and the first election was held on May 27, 1908, with Rev Thomas Hezmalhalch being elected as the first president of AFM in Africa.

It was the Apostolic Council, including Rev Chiangwa, that led the push to postpone elections, not the Madziyire faction. The draft document did not propose a succession plan. The CRP suggested a non-executive chairman at the assembly and province levels, who would be an elder, with day-to-day management remaining with pastors. This was intended to provide checks and balances, as a pastor cannot be accountable to the same board they chair.

A notable example of the issues that arose was in the Zhombe-Empress assembly, where outstanding balances for the pastor's salary would often occur whenever the pastor was transferred to a different assembly. The assembly would then pay the pastor for several months, claiming that they had not been paid. This was due to a lack of transparency and checks and balances, as the pastor served as both the chairmanship of the assembly and the signatory of the bank account. This concentration of power made it difficult for anyone to audit the chairman, who was also a respected pastor, until they left the assembly. Furthermore, the church board typically had no access to the treasurer's records, which were often kept in the pastor's office, creating an environment ripe for potential mismanagement.

The intervention of Professor Frank Chikane, the international leader of AFM, brought a temporary reprieve, but the underlying issues remained. The proposed constitutional reforms aimed to address issues like salary equalization and grading systems, but the process was marred by manipulation and power struggles. Ultimately, both factions demonstrated weaknesses in their approach, with a lack of transparency, trust, and clear communication. However, the Chiangwa faction showed strength in mobilizing support and bringing attention to the need for change, albeit in a way that may have been unconstitutional. The Madziyire faction demonstrated resilience and a willingness to adapt to changing circumstances. A balanced and inclusive approach was necessary to resolve the crisis and move the church forward.

28 April 2018

The Workers Council meeting, scheduled for April 28, 2018, had a clear agenda: to deliberate on the draft document and, if deemed necessary, pass the proposed constitutional amendments with or without modifications. The draft document had been extensively circulated to all church structures in both electronic and hard copy formats, ensuring widespread accessibility and transparency. However, the meeting was abruptly and unceremoniously terminated due to apparent preconceived notions and misunderstandings, which seemed to be orchestrated in advance. Regrettably, this premature termination meant that the proposed matters remained unresolved, leaving the constitutional review process in limbo. This unexpected turn of events raised concerns about the commitment to democratic governance and the willingness to engage in constructive dialogue within the church's leadership.

April 28, 2018, was a crucial date, designated not only for the Workers Council meeting but also for the elections of the Workers Council leadership, including provincial-level positions. However, the scheduling of both events on the same day without clear clarification caused confusion. In essence, April 28, 2018, marked the end of the three-year term for all office bearers, including the national executive committee, which had been elected in April 2015. The abrupt termination of the meeting resulted in a leadership vacuum, as the offices would remain vacant or be occupied by the previously elected members beyond their original term, potentially extending their tenure until later in 2018, the designated election year. This uncertainty raised concerns about the continuity of leadership and the potential impact on the church's governance and operations.

It is crucial to acknowledge that, up until April 28, 2018, the leadership of the Apostolic Faith Mission in Zimbabwe consisted of Aspher Madziyire as President, a position he held since the April 2015 elections. Cossam Chiangwa served as Deputy President, Amon Dubie Madawo as General Secretary, and Munyaradzi Shumba as the National Administrator, all of whom were also elected in April 2015.

Notably, the terms of office for these leaders expired on April 28, 2018, marking the end of their elected tenure. This expiration date is significant, as it raises questions about the legitimacy of any actions taken by these individuals beyond this point, particularly in relation to the disputed events that unfolded thereafter.

The clarity surrounding the expiration of their terms is essential for understanding the subsequent events and the challenges that arose within the church leadership.

It's essential to emphasize that, by law, an organization, including a government or a church, cannot exist in a vacuum without a leader, even during pending elections or other transitions. Typically, the president and cabinet ministers remain in office until the inauguration of the incoming president. Similarly, in the context of the Apostolic Faith Mission in Zimbabwe, if the President of the Church, Rev A Madziyire, were to step down due to an expired term, all other office bearers should also vacate their positions. This is because the President, Secretary, and Administrator are the primary office bearers, with the Deputy President serving in a supporting role.

It's crucial to note that Rev Madziyire and Cossam Chiangwa were both elected to the church leadership in April 2015, with their terms of office commencing and ending simultaneously. As per the church's constitution, they were to serve for three years, making their terms co-terminus. This means that if one's term expires, the other's does as well. The principle of contemporaneous terms ensures continuity and stability in leadership, preventing a power vacuum that could disrupt the organization's operations.

As a result, both Madziyire and Chiangwa were to continue serving in their respective positions until the scheduled election, which was to take place at any point during the year 2018. This meant that they would remain in office for the entirety of the election year, allowing for a smooth transition and ensuring continuity in leadership until the new elections could be held.

It's worth noting that this arrangement was likely made to maintain stability and avoid a power vacuum, given the significance of the positions held by Madziyire and Chiangwa. By allowing them to remain in office until the election, the organization could ensure that key responsibilities were still being attended to, and that the transition to new leadership would be managed in an orderly fashion.

The election year, 2018, was likely a critical period for the organization, with important decisions and changes on the horizon. By having both Madziyire and Chiangwa remain in office, the organization could benefit from their experience and expertise, even as it prepared for the transition to new leadership.

And so, despite the promising start, the meeting was abruptly terminated due to intense disagreements and heated debates from both sides of the council. Most members strongly advocated for the proposed changes, while a few, but influential, others vehemently opposed them. The discussions became increasingly polarized, with neither faction willing to concede or find common ground. It was clear that the meeting could not continue. As a result, the meeting failed to achieve its objectives, and no resolutions or decisions were made. The abrupt ending of the meeting left many issues unresolved, further exacerbating the existing tensions and power struggles within the organization. The lack of progress and the failure to address the long-standing problems only served to deepen the divisions, making it even more challenging to find a way forward.

CHAPTER eight

The Unconstitutional yet Court-Ordered Meeting

On July 18, 2018, Elder Tonderai Mathende successfully obtained a court order against the national office bearers of the Apostolic Faith Mission in Zimbabwe. The order, filed under case number HC 4756/18, directed the President and General Secretary to convene a National Workers Council meeting to address a critical agenda item that had been overlooked during the previous meeting on April 28, 2018. The motivations behind Elder Mathende's actions are unclear, but possibilities include a desire to restore order within the church, expedite the resolution of pending matters, or circumvent the six-month notice requirement for constitutional amendments. Regardless of his intentions, as a member of the church and a citizen, he had the right to seek legal recourse.

It is perplexing that the Church leadership, the respondents in this case, did not oppose the application. Perhaps they saw it as a convenient exit strategy, given the tumultuous aftermath of the aborted April 28, 2018 meeting. The prolonged debate over the draft constitution had created more adversaries than allies for the Executive. The emergence of unofficial groupings, such as the Pastors Fraternity and possibly the Elders Fraternity, had stirred up more chaos than harmony. Specifically, the Pastors Fraternity viewed the draft constitution as a threat, as it would prevent them from holding dual roles as pastors and chairmen of the Assembly Board.

Furthermore, some pastors had grown accustomed to exploiting their positions for personal gain, and the proposed centralization of funds and equal salary structures for similar roles did not sit well with them. Additionally, the introduction of rotation after five years at an assembly and the limitation of two five-year terms in elected posts were also met with resistance. It seemed that the quicker the amendments were passed, the better, as the existing tensions and power struggles within the Church leadership had become increasingly untenable. By not opposing the application, the Church leadership may have been attempting to expedite the process and bring a sense of closure to the contentious issues surrounding the draft constitution.

It is possible that the executive was in cahoots with Tonderai Mathende, but if so, they managed to conceal their alliance skillfully, leaving behind no discernible evidence of their collaboration. Alternatively, the Executive might have chosen not to oppose the application as a strategic decision to avoid further financial expenditure on what they perceived as frivolous matters. They may have anticipated a fierce resistance from the Pastors' Fraternity, led by influential figures like Pastor Mapingure, and opted to conserve resources rather than engage in a potentially protracted and costly legal battle.

By not opposing the application, the Executive may have sought to avoid exacerbating the existing tensions and conflicts within the Church, particularly with the Pastors' Fraternity. This decision could be seen as a pragmatic move to redirect their focus and resources towards more pressing issues, rather than getting entangled in a contentious and potentially divisive dispute. However, the true motivations behind the Executive's decision remain unclear, leaving room for speculation and interpretation.

Moreover, we must respect Elder Mathende's integrity, regardless of his motivations. As followers of Jesus Christ, we are encouraged to embody the wisdom and cunning of the serpent, while maintaining the innocence and gentleness of a dove, as stated in Matthew 10:16. This biblical principle emphasizes the importance of being strategic and discerning in our actions, while remaining true to our values and principles. By acknowledging Elder Mathende's right to seek legal recourse, we uphold the value of integrity and responsible action, even if his motivations are unclear. This approach allows us to navigate complex situations with wisdom and grace, just as Jesus taught.

The court's decision to uphold Elder Mathende's plea is significant, especially considering the unproductive outcome of the previous meeting. The judge's ruling demonstrated a commitment to ensuring that the church's internal processes are conducted in a fair and transparent manner. By granting the order, the court enabled the National Workers Council to reconvene and address the outstanding agenda item, potentially paving the way for greater clarity and resolution within the church's leadership.

It is worth noting that the court order was instrumental in bringing about this meeting, and its impact cannot be overstated. Had it not been for the court's intervention, the church's future would be shrouded in uncertainty, and the consequences of inaction would have been dire. The court order served as a catalyst, prompting the church to confront its internal struggles and work towards a resolution. In this sense, the September 15, 2018, Workers Council meeting was a turning point, marking a shift towards a new era of transparency, accountability, and governance within the church.

31 July 2018

In accordance with the court order issued under HC 4756/18 and a letter dated July 31, 2018, the President, Rev A Madziyire, convened a Workers' Council Meeting, scheduled for September 15, 2018. This meeting was a direct response to the court's directive, ensuring the church's compliance with the legal mandate. To facilitate a comprehensive review and discussion, both hard and soft copies of the draft constitution and amendment documents were disseminated to all church structures, mirroring the process undertaken on February 18, 2018.

This deliberate effort ensured that all stakeholders had access to the relevant documents, enabling them to engage meaningfully in the decision-making process. The distribution of documents in both physical and digital formats demonstrated the church's commitment to transparency and inclusivity, allowing members to scrutinize the proposed amendments and contribute to the constitutional review process. By doing so, the church leadership demonstrated its willingness to embrace democratic principles and foster a sense of ownership among its members, paving the way for a more collaborative and representative governance structure.

Furthermore, effective church governance is crucial, as it directly impacts the spiritual well-being of congregants. While the church is the body of Christ, not a democracy, certain aspects of church management can benefit from democratic principles. The Presbyterian Governance System strikes a balance between episcopal and congregational approaches, aligning with early church governance and theocratic principles. God created humans for rulership on His behalf, not democracy.

Church governance encompasses various aspects, similar to running a sound organization. With increasingly educated congregants, questions arise when management deviates from governance principles. Leaders often disregard church constitutions, exploiting the lack of civil and labor laws. The Council of Churches in the Sub-Saharan region found that 65% of congregants change denominations due to disagreements with church governance.

Therefore, church leaders must prioritize good governance, ensuring elected or appointed leaders are honorable, authoritative, and worthy. Popularity should not dictate leadership positions, as it can hinder effective governance. The story of Moses' twelve spies illustrates that majority opinions can be incorrect. Adherence to governing instruments is vital, as earthly decisions have heavenly implications.

When considering effective church governance, it's important to recognize that the church's human aspects, such as finances, administration, and management, can benefit from the application of democratic principles. However, theocratic governance ultimately prioritizes God's will over human desires, ensuring that spiritual guidance takes precedence over personal interests. To achieve this balance, governance structures should be designed to balance authority and accountability. Furthermore, educated congregants play a vital role in promoting improved governance by asking informed questions and advocating for transparency, ultimately contributing to a more effective and spiritually guided leadership.

By acknowledging these aspects, churches can strive for effective governance, ensuring the body of Christ remains a beacon of hope and spiritual growth.

Constitutions, regulations, and policies are essential for the effective governance of the visible church, providing a framework for management and administrative purposes. While these documents are guided by spiritual principles, they are not inherently spiritual themselves. Instead, they adhere to conventional governance principles, with democracy being the most widely accepted approach. The church, however, operates on two distinct levels: administrative and spiritual. It is crucial for these two wings to maintain mutual understanding and respect.

A notable example of this dynamic is the court case involving Elder Tonderai Mathende, which exclusively addressed administrative issues within the church. The case did not challenge spiritual aspects, such as doctrine or theological beliefs. In this context, it was imperative for the church's administrative wing to respect and comply with the court order. Similarly, the aborted meeting on April 28, 2018, was an administrative matter, unrelated to spiritual or doctrinal concerns.

In fact, the church's administrative wing has a responsibility to ensure that its actions align with both spiritual principles and legal requirements. By doing so, the church demonstrates its commitment to transparency, accountability, and good governance. This dual approach enables the church to maintain its spiritual integrity while navigating complex administrative and legal issues.

The church's administrative wing must navigate complex legal and governance issues while remaining true to its spiritual roots. However, when spiritual leaders prioritize administrative power over spiritual guidance, it can lead to a disconnect between the church's spiritual and administrative wings. This disconnect can result in a phenomenon where academic excellence is linked with spiritual profanity.

In such cases, church leaders may prioritize intellectual pursuits and administrative efficiency over spiritual growth and doctrinal integrity. This can lead to a hollowing out of the church's spiritual core, replacing it with a focus on worldly success and recognition. The consequences of such a shift can be far-reaching, ultimately undermining the church's credibility and spiritual authority.

To avoid this pitfall, church leaders must strike a delicate balance between academic excellence and spiritual integrity. They must prioritize spiritual guidance and doctrinal purity while still maintaining administrative competence and intellectual rigor. By doing so, the church can ensure that its spiritual and administrative wings work in harmony, promoting a vibrant and authentic Christian community.

In this context, our focus is on the church's administrative, academic, and managerial aspects, which are subject to the laws of the land and therefore fall under the jurisdiction of civil courts, hence the relevance of a court order.

CHAPTER Nine

Separated, We Understand; United, We Divide

As the conflicts within AFM Zimbabwe continued to escalate, Pastor George Mahlobo, the secretary general of AFM International, stepped in to address the situation. In a letter dated September 6, 2018, he expressed his deep concern that the internal struggles had reached a boiling point, threatening the very life, integrity, and credibility of AFM International.

With a sense of urgency, Pastor Mahlobo implored the Zimbabwean chapter to refrain from resorting to the courts to resolve their differences. Instead, he advocated for an out-of-court settlement agreement, hoping to avert the looming crisis.

Having assessed the situation, Pastor Mahlobo was convinced that the key players in the conflict were willing to go to great lengths to pursue their individual interests, even if it meant jeopardizing the well-being of the church. He believed that this relentless pursuit of power and control was hindering the move of the Holy Spirit within the church.

Determined to intervene, Pastor Mahlobo declared that AFM International was committed to stopping this destructive trajectory in the interest of both the Zimbabwean chapter and the global organization. He called upon all members and assemblies of AFM in Zimbabwe to unite in a 24-hour chain prayer, seeking divine intervention to guide the leadership towards a path that would save the church from division and ensure the continued pursuit of its ministry and mission.

15 September 2018

On September 15, 2018, the Workers Council convened and deliberated on the proposed Constitutional amendments. Following a thorough discussion, the council accepted the amendments, but with a significant caveat. In a surprising move, the council decided to suspend all provisions of the amended draft Constitution, except for those related to the conduct of elections. This suspension was intended to provide an opportunity for other church members to propose further amendments to the already amended draft Constitution.

The acceptance of the amendments, and the resolution to suspend was carried by an overwhelming majority of 3,440 votes in favor, with only 35 votes against, and no abstentions. Notably, the total number of councilors present was 3,475, indicating a high level of participation and engagement in the decision-making process. This unusual decision to suspend the amended draft Constitution raises questions about the council's intentions and the potential implications for the church's governance and operations.

However, upon closer examination, it becomes clear that the acceptance of the Constitutional amendments was largely a procedural move to facilitate progress, rather than a wholehearted endorsement of the proposed changes. In reality, several concerns and issues with the amendments remained unaddressed, necessitating further scrutiny and additional amendments to ensure the Constitution accurately reflected the needs and values of the church. The acceptance was, in essence, a temporary measure to keep the process moving forward, while also acknowledging that more work was needed to perfect the amendments.

However, the culmination of the CRP at the September 15, 2018, meeting demonstrated the church's commitment to democratic governance and its willingness to adapt to changing circumstances.

Nevertheless, a critical question arises: was the process of amending the constitution itself constitutional? Was the meeting where the amendments were considered even legal, given the Constitution governing the Church? We argue that it was not, and here's why.

The Church's constitution outlines specific requirements for passing a valid constitutional amendment, which are both cumulative and conjunctive.

Firstly, a six-month written notice must be given by either the Provincial Workers Council, the Apostolic Council, or both, to the General Secretary before the Workers Council meeting where the amendments will be considered.

Secondly, the notice must be accompanied by detailed proposals of the amendments.

Thirdly, both the notice and the detailed amendments must be sent to all Provincial Workers Councils before the meeting.

Lastly, the quorum for passing the amendment requires a two-thirds majority of the optimum membership of the Workers Council.

Given these stringent requirements, it appears that the process followed was flawed, casting doubt on the legitimacy of the amendments.

It is crucial to emphasize that the Workers Council, Apostolic Council, and office bearers were obligated to rigidly follow both the explicit provisions and underlying principles of the constitution. This adherence is particularly important, as legal courts typically interpret organizational constitutions, such as those of churches, in a similarly strict manner.

However, a detailed examination of the Workers Council meeting on September 15, 2018, reveals a striking inconsistency. The meeting was convened with only one month's notice, contrary to the constitution's stipulation of six months' notice. Moreover, the notice did not emanate from either the Workers Council or the Apostolic Council, as required by the constitution, but rather from the office bearers. Although the General Secretary distributed the notice and proposed amendments to the Provincial Councils for consideration at the next Workers Council meeting, the meeting's convening violated the constitution's clear requirements.

The failure to provide the requisite six months' notice and the improper origin of the notice render the meeting invalid. This oversight has far-reaching implications for the legitimacy of decisions made during the meeting, including the acceptance of Constitutional amendments.

As we grew older, we began to appreciate the complexity of certain professions, like law. We once wondered why becoming a lawyer required a minimum of three to four years of studying for a Bachelor of Laws degree, and why many individuals still choose to pursue this field despite its ancient roots. However, as we gained more insight, we realized that a lawyer's perspective is vastly different from our own. What initially seems like overwhelming evidence in support of a particular argument can quickly become overwhelming evidence against it if not carefully examined.

This nuanced understanding has taught us the importance of considering multiple viewpoints. Just as viewing something with both eyes provides a more comprehensive understanding than with one eye alone, analyzing a situation from different angles can reveal new insights. With this in mind, let's re-examine the Workers Council meeting of September 15, 2018, from a fresh perspective. By doing so, we may uncover aspects that were previously overlooked, and gain a deeper understanding of the events that transpired.

To begin with, it's essential to comprehend the underlying principles and values enshrined in the constitution of the Apostolic Faith Mission in Zimbabwe, in harmony with the teachings of the Word of God and the laws of the land. This understanding will provide a solid foundation for interpreting and applying the constitution's provisions effectively.

The constitution is the foundational document that delineates the purpose, objectives, governance structure, and decision-making processes of the church, as well as its relationship with its members. The preamble provides an introduction, stating the church's purpose and goals. This is followed by chapters that elaborately outline specific aspects of the church's structure and operations. These chapters cover various key areas, including the leadership structure, roles, and responsibilities, as well as the rights, privileges, and obligations of members. Additionally, they specify the authority and limitations of the church and its leaders, providing a clear framework for governance and decision-making.

Each chapter comprises sections that provide detailed provisions, ensuring clarity and precision. Additionally, the constitution establishes procedures for amending its contents, allowing for flexibility and adaptability.

As the supreme law of the church, the constitution is paramount, superseded only by the Word of God and biblically advocated laws of the land. In the event of any inconsistency between the constitution and other laws or regulations, the constitution prevails, and the conflicting law shall be deemed void to the extent of the inconsistency.

By serving as a foundation, the constitution guides the church's actions, decisions, and growth, ensuring accountability, stability, and continuity. Its provisions and principles promote unity, order, and harmony within the church, while also protecting the rights and interests of its members.

In this context, it is crucial to note that Rev. Madziyire, the President, and Rev. Madawo, the Secretary General, did not convene the Workers Council meeting on September 15, 2018, of their own volition. Instead, they acted in obedience to a court order issued in response to an unopposed application by Tonderai Mathende. The court's directive instructed them to convene the meeting with only 30 days' notice to the members of the Workers Council, with the 30-day period commencing within 7 days of serving the order on the last of the respondents cited.

This is significant, as it highlights that the meeting was convened under judicial duress, rather than at the discretion of the church leaders. Moreover, it is essential to recognize that the Constitution of the land takes precedence over all other constitutions, including that of the church. This means that the court's order, grounded in the national Constitution, superseded the church's constitution, which requires a six-month notice period for convening such a meeting. This unusual circumstance underscores the complexities and tensions that can arise when religious institutions intersect with civil law.

To eliminate any confusion, it's essential to acknowledge the legal principle which states that a court order, regardless of its underlying motivations or faith, carries legal weight and consequences. Unless successfully challenged and invalidated through proper legal channels, the order remains effective and binding, even if its legitimacy is disputed. This principle is crucial for maintaining the rule of law, as it prevents individuals from unilaterally disregarding laws they disagree with, simply by claiming they are invalid.

If this were not the case, and litigants were exempt from complying with laws pending their validity being determined, the legal system would descend into chaos. This would create an environment where anyone could challenge the validity of any law, not to seek justice, but to evade compliance or disrupt the legal process. The resulting confusion and disorder would render the application of the rule of law nearly impossible, undermining the very fabric of our legal system.

Within the framework of established legal principles, there exists a clear and absolute duty for every individual to comply with a court order issued by a competent jurisdiction, unless and until the order is formally set aside or discharged. This obligation is unwavering and uncompromising, applying even in situations where the affected person believes the order to be flawed, irregular, or potentially void. The person must still obey the order, despite any reservations or disagreements, until the order is officially overturned or invalidated through the proper legal channels. This strict requirement ensures the integrity and authority of the legal system, maintaining the rule of law and preventing individuals from unilaterally disregarding court decisions.

In the context of the Workers Council meeting on September 15, 2018, which deliberated on the proposed Constitutional amendments and accepted them with certain conditions, it is essential to acknowledge the meeting's validity from both a constitutional and biblical perspective. The meeting's decisions, including the acceptance of the amendments subject to the suspension of most provisions, except those related to election conduct, to allow for further member input, were in line with the church's governing principles.

From a biblical standpoint, it is important to recognize that God ordains earthly authorities, as stated in Romans 13:1-2. As long as the civil law does not conflict with godly principles, it is essential to respect and comply with it. In this case, the court order mandating the meeting's convening did not infringe upon any biblical teachings, and therefore, the meeting's actions were deemed valid.

Moreover, the meeting's decision to suspend most provisions, except those related to election conduct, demonstrated a commitment to inclusivity and member participation, aligning with biblical values of community and shared decision-making. By allowing further amendments, the council ensured that the Constitution would reflect the collective wisdom and input of the church members, rather than a select few.

Not only did the national executive board comply with the court order under case HC 4756/18, but a significant number of councilors also adhered to the directive. The executive reported an optimum number of 3,475 councilors, although some later disputed this figure, claiming it was actually 2,056.

Regardless of the exact number, over 2,000 individuals obeyed the court order and attended the extraordinary meeting, demonstrating a collective commitment to upholding the rule of law.

In hindsight, it can be argued that those who disagreed with the court order chose not to attend the meeting, thereby avoiding any potential complicity in its alleged illegality. Conversely, the presence of over 2,000 councilors at the meeting implies their tacit acceptance of the court's authority and the meeting's legitimacy. If the meeting were indeed illegal, then those who attended would be considered accomplices. Fortunately, the meeting was legal, and their participation was a testament to their dedication to the church's governance and adherence to the law.

The high attendance at the meeting underscores the importance of respecting court orders and the rule of law, even in cases where there may be disagreements or disputes. By complying with the court's directive, the councilors demonstrated their commitment to upholding the principles of justice and fairness, ensuring that the church's decision-making processes remain transparent, accountable, and legally sound.

Therefore, if anyone were to dispute the legitimacy of the Workers Council meeting, labeling it as illegal or unconstitutional, it should be those who chose not to attend the meeting who make such claims. After all, by abstaining from the meeting, they avoided any potential complicity in its alleged illegality.

Notwithstanding, the courts are equipped to address such grievances, and the judiciary will meticulously examine all aspects of the case. Through the rigorous scrutiny of both the applicants' lawyers and the defense attorneys, the truth will be revealed, and the court will render a verdict based on the evidence presented.

It is essential to have faith in the legal system, knowing that it provides a platform for resolving disputes and addressing concerns in a fair and impartial manner. The courts will carefully consider all arguments, evidence, and testimonies before making an informed decision. Ultimately, their ruling will provide clarity and closure on the matter, ensuring that justice is served and the rights of all parties are protected.

After all, Elder Tonderai Mathende played a significant role in convening the pivotal Workers Council meeting on September 15, 2018 - a gathering that proved to be a watershed moment in the church's history. This meeting, which can be likened to the eye of a storm, was the focal point of both harmony and discord, with far-reaching consequences that continue to shape the church's trajectory. Every aspect of this discussion revolves around this particular Council, underscoring its importance in the church's narrative.

20 September 2018

The Pastors Fraternity, which appeared to be a burgeoning faction within the church, adopted a resolution that would come to be known as the Gweru Declaration, on 20 September 2018. This move could be interpreted as an attempt to effectively repeal the existing constitution, potentially undermining the church's governance structure. The fact that the declaration was made outside of official church agendas and protocols suggests a level of defiance or contempt for the established order.

The Gweru Declaration may have been a manifestation of the growing tensions and power struggles within the church, particularly between the Pastors Fraternity and other factions or leadership groups. By issuing a declaration, the Pastors Fraternity may have been attempting to assert its influence and shape the church's future, potentially outside of the formal constitutional processes.

This development raises questions about the legitimacy and authority of the declaration, as well as its implications for the church's unity and governance. The fact that declarations are not typically part of church agendas adds to the perception that this move may have been a deliberate challenge to the status quo, rather than a constructive contribution to the church's decision-making processes.

21 September 2018

On September 21, 2018, the Apostolic Council convened to discuss and finalize the dates and guidelines for the upcoming triennial elections. The provincial elections were scheduled to take place on September 29 and October 3, 2018, followed by the national elections on November 3, 2018.

However, during the meeting, Deputy President Rev C Chiangwa announced his decision to part ways with the Executive Committee's way, citing his disagreement with the resolution passed by the Workers Council on September 15, 2018. He actually said he was going his own way, and stated that he could not accept the resolution, leading to his departure from the National Executive Committee.

After declaring his intention to go his own way, reportedly inspired by the Gweru Declaration, the Deputy President went on to show his muscles by issuing a written notice on September 20, 2018, announcing a Workers Council meeting to be held on September 22, 2018, at the Rufaro National Conference Center. This notice specifically targeted councilors who strongly opposed the Draft Document, viewing it as a significant departure from the church's traditional identity and values. The letter clarified that the upcoming meeting was exclusively for councilors who wished to remain part of the AFM in Zimbabwe Church, upholding the existing constitution that the September 15, 2018, meeting had attempted to replace.

In essence, this meeting was convened for councilors who rejected the constitutional changes and sought to preserve the church's status quo, governed by the current constitution. This development exposes the escalating divisions within the church, as the Deputy President and his supporters openly opposed the proposed reforms. By convening a separate meeting for like-minded councilors, they aimed to solidify their stance and potentially contest the decisions made during the September 15, 2018, meeting. This move highlights the intensity of the power struggle and the competing visions for the church's future, setting the stage for further conflict and potential fragmentation.

Looking closely, Deputy President Rev C Chiangwa's parting words, "I will go my own way," were ambiguous and open to interpretation. On one hand, he could have been signaling his intention to leave the church altogether, potentially due to disagreements with the recent resolution passed by the Workers Council. On the other hand, he might have been indicating a desire to take the church in a different direction, possibly at odds with the current leadership.

Alternatively, Rev Chiangwa's statement could have meant that he intended to address the issues at hand in a different manner, potentially through unconventional means. However, it is puzzling that he would aim to defy nearly one-hundred percent of councilors, who had democratically voted for the resolution. This raises questions about his intentions and methods.

In light of the Gweru meeting, which had taken place just a day earlier, it is possible that Rev Chiangwa was hinting at taking an unconstitutional approach to achieve his goals. This would be consistent with the tone and actions of the Gweru meeting, which had been perceived as a challenge to the church's established order. By "going his own way," Rev Chiangwa may have been signaling a willingness to bypass traditional channels and protocols, potentially leading to further conflict and division within the church.

If the situation escalates and the matter ends up in court, Rev Chiangwa's parting words could be used as evidence against him, potentially implicating him in a deliberate attempt to secede from the Church. His statement, "I will go my own way," could be interpreted as an open declaration of his intention to break away from the Church, with his words serving as a testament to his true intentions.

As the age-old adage goes, "the mouth speaks what the heart is full of." In this case, Rev Chiangwa's words may be seen as a reflection of his inner thoughts and feelings, revealing a desire to distance himself from the Church. If his actions align with his words, it could be argued that he has indeed seceded from the Church, with his statement serving as a public declaration of his decision.

In a court of law, such evidence could be used to support claims of Rev Chiangwa's secession, potentially leading to serious consequences for his future involvement with the Church. His words, once spoken, cannot be taken back, and may ultimately be used to hold him accountable for his actions.

However, the inclusion of the Deputy President's parting words in the legal proceedings would hinge on the decision of the applicants, the Executive Committee, to incorporate them into their founding affidavit. If the Executive Committee chooses to include Rev Chiangwa's statement, "I will go my own way," in their legal documentation, it could potentially be used as evidence against him in court.

The founding affidavit serves as the initial document submitted by the applicants to the court, outlining the facts and grounds for their case. By including Rev Chiangwa's parting words, the Executive Committee may aim to demonstrate his intention to secede from the Church, potentially strengthening their case against him.

On the other hand, if the Executive Committee decides not to include Rev Chiangwa's statement in their founding affidavit, it may not be considered as evidence in the legal proceedings. The court's decision would then be based solely on the facts and arguments presented in the affidavit, without reference to Rev Chiangwa's potentially incriminating words. Ultimately, the Executive Committee's decision on this matter would significantly impact the trajectory of the case.

However, Rev C Chiangwa's decision to convene a Workers Council through unconstitutional means may ultimately come back to haunt him. It appears that he may have predicated his actions on the September 15, 2018 meeting, which some individuals perceived as unconstitutional. Nevertheless, as previously clarified, that meeting was actually sanctioned by a court of law, thereby rendering it constitutional.

By relying on a potentially flawed understanding of the September 15 meeting, Rev Chiangwa may have inadvertently exposed himself to legal repercussions. His actions, deemed unconstitutional by some, could be seen as a misinterpretation of the court's ruling. This misunderstanding may lead to consequences, particularly if the court decides to scrutinize his decisions and actions in light of the constitutional framework.

Furthermore, Rev Chiangwa's reliance on a potentially unconstitutional precedent may undermine his credibility and legitimacy within the Church. If his actions are deemed unlawful, it could erode trust among Church members and leaders, ultimately affecting his ability to effectively lead and make decisions. The consequences of his actions may prove far-reaching, highlighting the importance of adhering to constitutional guidelines and respecting the rule of law.

22 September 2018

Despite Rev A Madziyire's cease and desist order, the attendees proceeded with the meeting on September 22, 2018, which had far-reaching and profound consequences. The contentious gathering, allegedly attended by 2,056 councilors (comprising 1,562 delegates and 567 pastors from 513 assemblies, with 137 assemblies tendering apologies for their absence), scrutinized and nullified the resolution passed on September 15, 2018. By an overwhelming majority of 1,557 votes, the attendees ousted the serving national office bearers, except for Deputy President Rev C Chiangwa.

The meeting's attendees then assumed the authority to conduct triennial elections on October 6, 13, and 20, 2018, and incited members to revolt against the removed office bearers. This marked a pivotal moment in the church's history, leading to a deepening rift and a parallel electoral process that contravened the official elections scheduled by the church's leadership. The actions taken during this meeting would have significant and lasting implications for the church's unity, governance, and future direction, setting the stage for further conflict and division.

Let's take it again, slowly. On September 22, 2018, Chiangwa's faction convened a meeting of the Workers' Council, which passed a vote of no confidence in the sitting church executive, with the notable exception of Chiangwa himself, who had been serving as the Deputy President since 2015. This move raises several questions about Chiangwa's authority and the legitimacy of his actions. It appears that Chiangwa assumed sweeping powers to approbate and reprobate, but the source of this authority remains unclear.

If Chiangwa was indeed subject to the law like everyone else, it is puzzling that he believed he could continue to serve as Deputy President beyond April 28, 2018, while claiming that the terms of the other executive members had expired. This inconsistency raises questions about his jurisdiction to act on behalf of the church after that date.

Moreover, Chiangwa's tenure as Deputy President from 2015 to September 22, 2018, seems to contradict his assertion that the terms of the other executive members had lapsed. If he was still serving in his role, who was he deputizing if the president's term had allegedly expired? And with whom was he working if the terms of the rest of the Executive had supposedly expired?

Furthermore, on September 20, 2018, Reverend Cossum Chiangwa issued a memo addressed to all Apostolic Faith Mission (AFM) Overseers, Pastors, Elders, and Deacons. There is a critical distinction between the roles of Elders, Pastors, and Deacons, who hold ministerial offices based on their spiritual calling, and Overseers, who are pastors elected to serve as head pastors and chairmen of their respective provinces. In this context, the terms of office for elected members, such as Overseers and other executive members, including Madziyire, Madawo, and Shumba, who were elected in 2015, had expired on April 28, 2018.

These anomalies and contradictions will likely not escape the scrutiny of the courts. The judiciary will need to examine the legality and validity of Chiangwa's actions, including his convening of the extraordinary Workers Council meeting on September 22, 2018. The courts will likely seek to clarify the extent of Chiangwa's authority and the legitimacy of his claims, particularly in light of these glaring inconsistencies.

Examining the situation from an alternative perspective, the letter dated September 20, 2018, extended an invitation to councilors who believed that those who accepted the draft document, with the exception of the election-related aspects, had effectively seceded from the church. This raises a critical question: if these individuals had indeed seceded, why would a vote of no confidence be necessary against them? The act of voting them out through a no-confidence motion implies that Rev Madziyire and others were still considered part of the church and held their offices until September 22, 2018, as per the resolution adopted during the September 22 meeting.

The inconsistency becomes apparent when considering the timeline of events. If the vote of no confidence occurred on September 22, 2018, it contradicts the claim that these individuals had seceded from the church on September 15, 2018. This discrepancy suggests confusion within the shadow executive formed on September 22, 2018. By attempting to remove individuals through a vote of no confidence, the group implicitly acknowledged their continued membership and leadership roles within the church, undermining their earlier assertion of secession.

Furthermore, this paradox highlights potential flaws in the reasoning and decision-making processes of the shadow executive. If they genuinely believed that Rev Madziyire and others had seceded, it would be illogical to subsequently vote them out, as this action would only be applicable to members still within the church. This inconsistency may indicate a lack of clarity or cohesion within the group, potentially weakening their position and credibility.

If the matter is brought before the courts, and the sitting Executive Committee incorporates these flaws into their founding affidavit, Rev Chiangwa and his team may face significant challenges. The inclusion of self-contradicting statements, which imply falseness and unreliability, could severely undermine their case.

In legal proceedings, consistency and credibility are crucial. When a party's statements or actions are contradictory, it can raise doubts about their truthfulness and trustworthiness. In this instance, the inconsistencies in Rev Chiangwa's team's narrative may be used as evidence against them, potentially leading to a loss of credibility and a weakening of their position.

Furthermore, the courts may view these self-contradicting statements as an attempt to mislead or deceive, which could result in adverse inferences being drawn against Rev Chiangwa and his team. This could ultimately impact the court's decision, potentially leading to a ruling in favor of the sitting Executive Committee.

It is essential for Rev Chiangwa and his team to address these inconsistencies and clarify their position to maintain credibility and build a strong case. Failure to do so may result in significant legal consequences, highlighting the importance of careful planning, consistent messaging, and attention to detail in legal proceedings.

Meanwhile, the ousted Madziyire is adamant that the 'coup' was illegal and he will be approaching the high court to nullify the outcome of the gathering.

CHAPTER ten

The Battle for Legitimacy and Control

On September 25, 2018, the Apostolic Council convened and made a significant decision to set aside the proposed electoral amendments. This move was necessitated by the fact that the amendments were fundamentally incompatible with the preserved governance structures outlined in the amended draft constitution. It is crucial to note that the September 15, 2018, meeting had a singular purpose: to conclude the unfinished business of the aborted April 28, 2018, meeting, as directed by the court. In essence, the September 15 meeting was a continuation of the April 28 meeting, and its agenda was limited to completing the unfinished business. The September 25 meeting, therefore, took a step back to re-evaluate the proposed electoral amendments in light of the preserved governance structures. Upon review, it became clear that the amendments were in complete dissonance with the established governance framework, leading the Apostolic Council to abandon them. This decision highlighted the complexities and challenges inherent in reconciling the proposed reforms with the existing constitutional framework.

This move effectively suspended all amendments accepted on September 15, 2018, pending further review, input, and scrutiny from councilors.

While the motivations behind this decision are not explicitly stated, it is possible that the Apostolic Council was responding to concerns raised by the Chiangwa faction. The council may have been attempting to address the faction's discomfort with the amendments, potentially in an effort to facilitate their return to the fold. However, despite this olive branch, the Chiangwa faction seemed resolute in their decision to pursue a separate path.

By abandoning the electoral amendments, the Apostolic Council may have been seeking to create an opportunity for reconciliation and unity. Nevertheless, the Chiangwa faction's apparent determination to forge ahead with their own agenda suggests that the rift within the church was more profound than initially thought. This development sets the stage for further conflict and raises questions about the long-term implications for the church's governance and unity.

The Apostolic Council's decision to abandon the electoral amendments may have been a strategic move to prepare for potential legal proceedings, anticipating that the dispute could escalate into a court battle. The September 22, 2018, meeting convened by the Anti-reform faction seemed to set the stage for a contentious legal showdown. By establishing a rival Workers Council, Apostolic Council, and Executive Committee, the Anti-reform side was asserting its legitimacy and claiming authority, potentially creating a parallel governance structure.

In response, the pro-reform faction may have been attempting to establish a paper trail and narrative to support their claims in a potential court case. By doing so, they could argue that their actions were legitimate, inclusive, tolerant, and constitutional, despite the Deputy President's non-recognition of their meeting and decisions. This move could enable them to counter the rival councils' and committees' claims of parallel authority, which could be used to challenge the official leadership's legitimacy in court.

This development could lead to a complex and contentious legal dispute, with both sides presenting arguments and evidence to support their claims of legitimacy. The court would need to navigate the intricacies of the dispute, considering the validity of each side's claims and the implications for the organization's governance and unity.

In response to the Anti-reformist faction's narrative that the pro-reformists had adopted the amended draft constitution and thereby seceded from the church to form a new entity, distinct from the authentic AFM in Zimbabwe, the Madziyire faction appeared to be strategically countering this claim. By abandoning the electoral amendments and re-establishing their commitment to the original constitution, the pro-reformists aimed to debunk the Anti-reformist faction's allegations.

The Anti-reformist faction had been disseminating a narrative that the pro-reformists' adoption of the amended draft constitution constituted a de facto secession from the church, resulting in the formation of a new organization that merely shared the AFM name. However, the Madziyire faction's actions suggested a calculated move to undermine this narrative and assert their legitimacy as the authentic representatives of the AFM in Zimbabwe.

By re-affirming their allegiance to the original constitution, the pro-reformists sought to demonstrate their commitment to the church's founding principles and values, thereby challenging the Anti-reformist faction's claims of their supposed secession. This strategic maneuvering highlighted the intense power struggle within the church, with both factions engaged in a battle for legitimacy, authority, and control.

26 September 2018

Following the abandonment of the electoral amendments accepted during the September 15, 2018, court-ordered meeting, the sitting Executive Committee, led by the Madziyire faction, extended an olive branch to the renegade Chiangwa faction on September 26, 2018. They urged the dissenting brethren to rejoin the mainstream fold, effectively reversing their decision to secede. However, the Chiangwa faction declined this offer, indicating their resolve to pursue a separate path.

This development could be seen as a strategic move by the Madziyire faction to establish a paper trail and demonstrate their willingness to reconcile, potentially strengthening their position in impending court proceedings. It was likely apparent to the Madziyire faction that the Chiangwa faction had already made up their minds and would not return to the fold, making the offer a symbolic gesture rather than a genuine attempt at reconciliation.

By extending this offer, the Madziyire faction may have been attempting to create a narrative that they were open to reconciliation, while the Chiangwa faction was obstinate and unwilling to compromise. This could be used to their advantage in a court of law, where the Madziyire faction could argue that they had taken reasonable steps to resolve the dispute amicably, but were rebuffed by the Chiangwa faction.

In stark contrast, the Chiangwa faction rebuffed the cease and desist order and the call to return to the mainstream fold issued by the Madziyire faction.

Instead, they took a provocative step by appointing their own 26 provincial overseers and a national administrator, to whom church funds were to be remitted. This move was a clear assertion of their parallel authority and a direct challenge to the Madziyire faction's leadership. Furthermore, they urged all church members to disregard the triennial dates set by the Apostolic Council, effectively calling for a boycott of the official church events.

Notably, the Chiangwa faction's appointment of 26 provincial overseers reveals a significant detail about the level of support for the Reform Side. Out of the 32 provincial overseers in the Apostolic Council, only 6 had aligned themselves with the Deputy President, Rev C Chiangwa. This small group comprised Rev Chiangwa himself, his deputy Rev Amon Chinyemba, the general secretary Dr Rev Nathan Nhira, and three other individuals.

This stark numerical disparity indicates that the majority of the Apostolic Council members had not supported Rev Chiangwa's faction. The appointment of 26 new provincial overseers by the Chiangwa faction, mostly comprising deputy overseers, raises important questions about the legitimacy and authority of these appointments. If the Madziyire faction chooses to raise this issue in their legal challenge, the courts may need to consider the implications of these appointments and whether they constitute a valid exercise of authority within the church's governance structure. This could potentially impact the outcome of the legal dispute and the future leadership of the church.

On the same date, Deputy President Rev C Chiangwa wrote to the Madziyire faction, informing them of the misconduct charges leveled against them. These charges stemmed from their acceptance of the constitutional amendments, which the Chiangwa faction deemed illegitimate. Rev Chiangwa stated that the charges originated from the Workers Council meeting held on September 22, 2018, which had been convened by the Anti-reformist faction. This letter served as a formal notification of the disciplinary action taken against the Madziyire faction, further escalating the conflict within the church. By taking these actions, the Chiangwa faction demonstrated their determination to establish a parallel governance structure, rivaling the official leadership of the church. This move would likely lead to a protracted and contentious legal battle, with both factions vying for control and legitimacy within the church.

Moreover, the Chiangwa faction disseminated a memorandum on September 26, 2018, claiming that their meeting on September 22, 2018, had successfully pressured the Madziyire Apostolic Council into abandoning the electoral amendments. This assertion may be true or false, but it underscored the Chiangwa faction's defiance and refusal to reconcile with the mainstream fold, as urged by the sitting Executive Committee. By circulating this memorandum, the Chiangwa faction aimed to bolster their narrative that their actions had achieved a significant victory, forcing the Madziyire faction to retreat from their proposed reforms. This move was likely intended to galvanize support among their followers and reinforce their position as a legitimate authority within the church.

However, it is essential to note that this claim may be disputed, and the actual motivations behind the Madziyire Apostolic Council's decision to abandon the electoral amendments might be more complex. Nevertheless, the Chiangwa faction's memorandum served as a public declaration of their triumph and a reaffirmation of their commitment to their parallel governance structure, further entrenching the divisions within the church.

27 September 2018

On September 27, 2018, the situation escalated further when the Deputy President, Chiangwa, and his supporters rejected the offer of reconciliation. In response, the church leadership suspended Chiangwa and his lieutenants without pay and benefits, citing their involvement in an unauthorized meeting and their alleged role in stirring up rebellion, disharmony, confusion, destabilization, disorder, and disturbances within the church.

The charges leveled against them included participating in an illegal meeting on September 22, 2018, which was not sanctioned by the official leadership, and fomenting rebellion and opposition against the legitimate leadership of the church. They were also accused of creating disharmony, confusion, and disorder among the membership, destabilizing the church and its operations, forming a splinter group, and attempting to usurp the powers of the Apostolic Council and other office bearers in violation of the church's constitution and governance structures.

These charges suggested that the church leadership viewed Chiangwa's actions as a serious threat to the stability and unity of the organization, and were determined to take decisive action to maintain order and discipline. The suspensions and charges marked a significant escalation of the conflict, and set the stage for further legal and administrative battles.

And so, the sitting Executive Committee took decisive action by issuing individual letters to each of the Chiangwa Executives who had been unlawfully appointed on September 22, 2018, or thereafter. The letters notified them of their immediate suspension without pay or benefits, effective from the date of the letter.

The suspended executives were summoned to appear before a disciplinary hearing authority to respond to allegations of misconduct, as outlined in the Labour (National Employment Code of Conduct) Regulations, 2006, in conjunction with the church's constitution. The primary allegations against them were their participation in an unauthorized meeting held at Rufaro Centre on September 22, 2018, which yielded outcomes detrimental to the church's objectives.

This move by the sitting Executive Committee aimed to address the illegitimate appointments and actions of the Chiangwa faction, while also upholding the church's constitution and governance structures. By invoking disciplinary measures, the committee sought to restore order and accountability within the church.

Conversely, Nathan Nhira, the shadow-church Secretary General of the Chiangwa faction, penned another letter announcing the appointment of new overseers for the church. This move was a brazen attempt to supplant the existing overseers, who had been democratically elected by the church members. The newly appointed overseers were mostly former Deputy

Overseers in their respective provinces, a clear indication of the faction's intention to consolidate power and control.

This development was fraught with abnormalities. Firstly, the appointments contravened the church's constitution, which explicitly stated that overseers were to be elected from among pastors, not appointed. By disregarding this fundamental principle, the Chiangwa faction demonstrated their willingness to manipulate the church's governance structure to suit their interests.

Furthermore, Nhira's letter appeared to defy the official leadership's suspension of the Chiangwa faction, which they claimed had been illegitimately imposed. This move was a clear challenge to the authority of the church's leadership and a deliberate attempt to create a parallel governance structure. The letter served as a public declaration of the faction's intention to operate outside the bounds of the church's constitution and disregard the legitimacy of the official leadership.

The developments on this day revealed a strategic escalation by the Madziyire faction, as they methodically built a case against the Chiangwa faction. Conversely, the Anti-reform side, led by Chiangwa, appeared to be intensifying their propaganda efforts, leveraging the church's main media channels to disseminate information favoring their narrative. Social media platforms were flooded with damning allegations against the Madziyire faction, portraying them as the primary aggressors in the conflict.

Notably, the Chiangwa faction seemed oblivious to the impending legal showdown, despite the Madziyire faction's deliberate and calculated moves to establish a paper trail and gather evidence. The suspension letters and disciplinary hearings initiated by the Madziyire faction were clear indications of their preparation for a legal battle, yet the Chiangwa faction appeared to be focused solely on swaying public opinion through their propaganda machinery.

This disconnect suggested that the Chiangwa faction might be underestimating the Madziyire faction's resolve and legal acumen, potentially leaving them vulnerable to a decisive legal challenge. As the situation continued to unfold, it became increasingly evident that the conflict was far from a simple power struggle, but rather a complex and multifaceted dispute with far-reaching implications for the church's governance and future.

28 September 2018

On September 28, 2018, AFM International president Pastor Frank Chikane intervened in the ongoing church dispute by sending a circular to all AFM presidents, providing guidance on resolving the issues within AFM in Zimbabwe.

Pastor Frank Chikane directed that the AFM Zimbabwe apostolic council should finalize the constitution amendments by January 2019, emphasizing the importance of inclusivity in the process. He stressed that no one should feel that the proposed amendments were being imposed without considering their views, and he encouraged all parties to work together, with divine guidance, to implement the decisions and maintain the unity of the church during the reform process.

14 October 2018

On 14 October 2018, the Staff Reporter of The Zimbabwe Mail reported that Dr. Madziyire's group is known as the "Reform AFM," while Rev. Chiangwa's camp is referred to as the "Original AFM." According to the report, Rev. Chiangwa's camp is adhering to the original constitution of the church. The report also stated that Rev. Chiyangwa's team held provincial elections on 6 and 13 October 2018 to choose new leadership in preparation for national executive elections, while Dr. Madziyire's camp planned to hold polls on December 31, 2018.

However, the accuracy of the report is questionable. It appears that the reporter may have been presented with propaganda, and failed to verify the authenticity of the information before publishing. Furthermore, it is surprising that the chief editor did not catch these flaws.

Contrary to the report, the Madziyire group had announced all election dates at the Apostolic Council meeting on 21 September 2018, which Rev. C. Chiangwa attended. The final day of elections was set for 3 November 2018, not 31 December 2018, which was actually the last day of the election year (1 January to 31 December 2018).

As was the trend of propaganda during that era, which unfortunately persists to this day, it was not unexpected for readers to come across such misinformation online. Social media platforms were flooded with all sorts of derogatory content and false information aimed at discrediting the Madziyire faction, making it challenging to discern fact from fiction.

This type of propaganda creates a false sense of security among supporters of the perpetrators, leading to overconfidence and complacency. As a result, they may underestimate their opponents and fail to prepare adequately, ultimately leading to unexpected outcomes on the day of reckoning.

The Bible teaches us that our actions have consequences, and we will reap what we sow (Galatians 6:7-8). This principle is echoed in Luke 6:38, which states, "Give, and it will be given to you. A good measure, pressed down, shaken together and running over, will be poured into your lap. For with the measure you use, it will be measured to you." This means that our generosity and kindness will be reciprocated in abundance.

However, the converse is also true. If we sow discord, strife, and division, we can expect to reap a harvest of conflict and turmoil (Proverbs 16:28). As the Bible warns, "Whoever sows injustice will reap calamity" (Proverbs 22:8). When we spread rumors, gossip, or engage in divisive behavior, we create an environment conducive to conflict and reap the consequences of our actions.

In the context of the AFM church dispute, this principle is particularly relevant. The propagation of misinformation and the sowing of discord have led to a climate of mistrust and division. As the Bible cautions, "A perverse person stirs up conflict, and a gossip separates close friends" (Proverbs 16:28). If we fail to address these issues and instead continue to sow discord, we can expect to reap a harvest of conflict and strife.

In contrast, if we choose to sow seeds of love, kindness, and understanding, we can expect to reap a harvest of peace and unity (Galatians 5:22-23). As the Bible encourages, "Let us therefore make every effort to do what leads to peace and to mutual edification" (Romans 14:19). By embracing this approach, we can create an environment conducive to reconciliation and restoration.

10 January 2019

Chiangwa and four others filed a court application (HC 179/19) on January 10, 2019, seeking a declaratory order to be recognized as the duly elected office bearers of the church. However, their actions raise questions about their legitimacy and timing. They held parallel elections in October 2018 and filed the application four months after the events in question, challenging the outcomes of September 15, 2018.

The court may scrutinize the technicalities of their case, probing the legitimacy of their executive to address past events when they lacked authority. The delay in filing the application and potential implications of retroactive decision-making may also be investigated.

Furthermore, the court may seek clarity on whether Chiangwa's actions were in accordance with the constitution when he convened meetings on September 22, 2018. If the meeting was unconstitutional, it could render all subsequent actions, including the court application, invalid. This would mean Chiangwa and his team lack the authority to challenge the sitting executive in court. The courts will need to consider these critical questions to determine the validity of Chiangwa's claims and the legitimacy of his faction's actions.

CHAPTER eleven

Vulnerable Congregants Caught in Crossfire

On February 4, 2019, the Madawo faction took legal action to prevent the Chiyangwa faction from holding meetings at Rufaro, including the upcoming Widows and Single Mothers (WISMO) annual conference scheduled for that weekend. They sought a High Court order to halt these meetings until the pending court case in the High Court was resolved.

This move aimed to prevent the Chiyangwa faction from proceeding with their planned events, including the WISMO conference, which was just days away. By seeking a court order, the Madawo faction hoped to maintain the status quo and prevent any actions that could potentially prejudice the outcome of the pending court case.

The WISMO conference was likely to be a significant event, bringing together widows and single mothers from various provinces, and the Madawo faction's legal action may have been intended to prevent the Chiyangwa faction from using this event to further their own interests or gain an advantage in the dispute.

7 February 2019

The High Court issued an injunction, blocking the Chiyangwa faction from hosting their annual Widows and Single Mothers' conference at the Rufaro Conference Centre in Chatsworth, following legal action initiated by the faction led by Reverend Amon Madawo. The court order, dated February 7, 2019, specifically prohibited the Chiyangwa faction and their congregants from convening any conferences, meetings, or related activities in the name of the AFM in Zimbabwe Church at the Rufaro Conference Centre in Masvingo.

The court order read: "The respondents and all those congregants under the first respondent's church are ordered not to convene any conferences or meetings or any related activities in the name of AFM in Zimbabwe Church or otherwise at the Rufaro Conference Centre in Masvingo until the matter pending before this court, case No. 9129/18, is finalized."

This ruling effectively halted the Chiyangwa faction's plans to hold the WISMO conference, which was scheduled to take place at Rufaro Conference Centre. The court's decision ensured that the status quo was maintained until the pending court case was resolved, preventing any actions that could have potentially prejudiced the outcome of the dispute.

However, preparations for the conference were at an advanced stage, with many congregants having already traveled significant distances to attend. Some had departed from their homes, with a few coming from as far as 300 km away, while others had already arrived at Rufaro. Typically, conferences at Rufaro begin on Thursday evening, with congregants camping on site before sundown, although many more arrive during the night and on Friday morning.

The court order, issued right on the day the conference was set to begin, was likely to cause a chaotic and distressing scene. The sudden cancellation of the event would not only dash the hopes of innocent congregants who had invested time, money, and effort into attending but also lead to financial losses and further escalate the already tense situation.

The conflict between the two factions, likened to two bulls fighting, would ultimately be the grass that suffers the most - the innocent congregants caught in the middle. Many would be left feeling morally distressed, with their expectations shattered and their resources depleted. The court order would only serve to intensify the infighting, causing more harm to the very people the church was meant to serve.

In all wars, including the factional disputes within the Apostolic Faith Mission in Zimbabwe, not everyone is initially an interested party. Typically, only a small group of individuals, driven by personal interests and ambitions, spark the conflict. The majority of congregants, however, are often drawn into the conflict through politicking and manipulation.

These individuals, often unaware of the true motives of the conflict's instigators, are sold a false narrative that serves only to further the interests of the few. The congregants, carrying the heavy burden of the conflict, are left to bear the consequences of the power struggles, while the true beneficiaries of the war reap the rewards.

In the case of the AFM in Zimbabwe, it was evident that the general congregants were misled and exploited, unaware of the underlying motivations and agendas driving the conflict. The factional leaders, seeking to advance their own interests, preyed on the trust and loyalty of their followers, using them as pawns in their struggle for power and control. Meanwhile, the majority of congregants were left to suffer the consequences of the conflict, their spiritual well-being and sense of community compromised by the infighting.

As the Bible says, "For nothing is secret that will not be revealed, nor anything hidden that will not be known and come to light" (Luke 8:17). This scripture reminds us that all secrets, no matter how well-hidden, will eventually be exposed. The darkness will be illuminated, and the truth will be revealed.

In the context of the Apostolic Faith Mission in Zimbabwe's leadership dispute, this scripture serves as a warning to those who have engaged in deceitful and manipulative tactics to further their own interests. God, who stands up for His people when the time is ripe, will not be mocked. He will expose the secrets and lies, and bring to light the truth.

Furthermore, as Jesus warned in Matthew 7:22-23, some individuals will attempt to justify their actions, claiming to have done great works in God's name. However, if their actions were motivated by selfish ambition and a desire for power, rather than a genuine love for God and His people, they will be sent away from His presence, labeled as "sons of Belial" (2 Corinthians 6:15). This serves as a stark reminder that true faith is not about seeking power or recognition but about serving God with humility and integrity.

Some revelations of the hidden truths surrounding the Apostolic Faith Mission in Zimbabwe's leadership dispute will not wait until Judgment Day. Soon, the true culprits will be exposed, and either the Madawo faction or the Chiyangwa faction will be proven responsible for the conflict. While the courts of law may deliver their verdicts, the Holy Spirit will ultimately confirm or discredit the judgments.

As the Bible says, "You will know them by their fruits" (Matthew 7:16). The actions and behaviors of both factions will be laid bare for all to see, revealing their true intentions and character. If the Reform-Side is false, they will likely abandon the reforms in a way that will be perceived as a clear indication of

God's disapproval. On the other hand, if the Anti-Reform side is at fault, they will likely disregard the constitution they claim to uphold, and a few individuals will unconstitutionally amend it, exposing their true motives and revealing that the reforms were not the root cause of the dispute.

In either case, the truth will be revealed, and the fruits of both factions will be plain for all to see. The situation will become so clear that it will be evident that God's hand is at work, guiding the outcome and revealing the true culprits. Ultimately, the truth will prevail, and justice will be served.

The Bible talks much about Widows, God Himself standing as their husband and father. Mistreating Widows must not be on the leaders' agenda.

While the Madawo faction may be perceived as the antagonists in this situation, it is essential to note that the court order was not specifically targeted at the Widows' conference, but rather at all gatherings of the Chiyangwa faction at Rufaro. This was a broader legal battle, and as with any conflict, there are often innocent victims caught in the crossfire. In this case, the Widows and Single Mothers who were scheduled to attend the conference became unintended casualties of the dispute.

It is also important to acknowledge that the Chiyangwa faction had an opportunity to seek legal recourse before their meeting on September 22, 2018, regarding the controversial constitutional amendments. However, by choosing not to pursue this option and instead taking matters into their own hands, they inadvertently contributed to the escalation of the conflict.

Taking the law into one's own hands can be seen as a sign of disrespect towards both one's opponent and the legal system as a whole. This approach often leads to further conflict and, ultimately, harm to innocent parties. In this instance, the Widows and Single Mothers, who were likely unaware of the intricacies of the dispute, became the unintended victims of the power struggle between the two factions.

8 February 2019

On February 8, 2019, Reverend Chiyangwa took his appeal against the High Court's decision to the Supreme Court, seeking to overturn the ruling that had blocked his faction's events at Rufaro. However, on the very same day, Reverend Madawo made an urgent application to the High Court, seeking a stay of execution to halt the Chiyangwa faction's planned events. Unfortunately for Reverend Madawo, the court denied his request, paving the way for the Chiyangwa faction to proceed with their scheduled activities.

Seizing the opportunity, the Chiyangwa faction went ahead with their Widows and Single Mothers (WISMO) Conference, which took place on Saturday, February 9, and concluded on Sunday, February 10, 2019. Despite the ongoing legal battles and disputes, the conference proceeded without interruption, allowing the attendees to gather and participate in the event as planned. The successful hosting of the conference was seen as a significant victory for the Chiyangwa faction, even as the legal drama continued to unfold.

The Chiyangwa faction's decision to appeal the court order to the Supreme Court was a wise move, as it allowed for a higher authority to review the decision and potentially overturn it. The Supreme Court's acceptance of Rev Chiyangwa's plea was also prudent, given the sensitive nature of religious matters and their potential to spark volatility if not handled carefully.

While the Madawo side, also known as the Madziyire side, had sought a declaratur, which is a legal declaration of rights, the appeal lodged by Rev Chiyangwa prevented the stay of execution sought by Rev Madawo. This was significant, as it allowed the Chiyangwa faction to proceed with their planned events, including the Widows and Single Mothers Conference.

Moreover, the Supreme Court's decision to hear the appeal demonstrated its commitment to protecting the country's integrity and upholding the moral fabric of society. By intervening in this dispute, the court helped to prevent potential unrest and ensured that the rights of all parties involved were protected. This was particularly important, given the potential for religious conflicts to escalate and have far-reaching consequences.

In essence, the Supreme Court's actions in this case demonstrated a deep understanding of the complexities of religious disputes and the need for careful handling to prevent harm to individuals and society as a whole. By accepting Rev Chiyangwa's appeal and preventing the stay of execution, the court helped to maintain social cohesion and protect the country's integrity.

While many neutral Christians may wonder why Reverend Madawo and his team sought a stay of execution, despite knowing it would cause significant distress to the congregants already gathered at Rufaro, including senior citizens, it is essential to consider the complexities of the situation. The fact that thousands of people supported the Chiyangwa cause, while thousands others disagreed with it, meant that Reverend Madawo also had a substantial support base. These supporters were the very congregants that the leaders had a responsibility to protect and care for.

By seeking a stay of execution, Reverend Madawo was likely trying to demonstrate his commitment to his followers and show that he was willing to take action to defend their interests. Had he not done so, he risked disheartening a significant number of his supporters, potentially leading some to lose faith and abandon the cause. In essence, Reverend Madawo was trying to maintain the trust and confidence of his followers by taking a stand, even if it meant going against the Chiyangwa faction.

Moreover, Reverend Madawo had already started down this path by opposing the Chiyangwa faction, and it was natural for him to see it through to its conclusion. To have done otherwise would have been seen as a sign of weakness or lack of resolve, potentially damaging his reputation and credibility among his supporters. By seeking a stay of execution, Reverend Madawo was, in effect, trying to protect his flock and maintain the integrity of his leadership.

This age-old adage, "Stop the War!", resonates deeply across the globe, transcending cultures and generations. It serves as a poignant reminder of the devastating consequences of conflict, which ravages not only the combatants but also innocent bystanders, leaving destruction and despair in its wake. War annihilates everything in its path, sparing neither lives nor livelihoods, and leaving deep scars that can take years to heal.

The indiscriminate nature of war is a stark reality, as it destroys homes, communities, and entire cities, displacing families and shredding the fabric of society. The physical toll is catastrophic, with countless lives lost, and many more irreparably harmed. The emotional and psychological impact is equally profound, as survivors grapple with trauma, grief, and the loss of loved ones.

Furthermore, war disrupts the social, economic, and cultural foundations of affected regions, plunging communities into chaos and poverty. The environment, too, suffers irreparable damage, as natural resources are exploited and ecosystems are ravaged. The reverberations of war are felt far beyond the battlefield, causing widespread suffering and destabilization.

In the context of the Apostolic Faith Mission in Zimbabwe's leadership dispute, the "Stop the War!" adage takes on added significance. The conflict, though not a traditional war, has already caused harm to the church community, with reputations tarnished, relationships strained, and the faith of some shaken. By echoing the call to "Stop the War!", we acknowledge the urgent need for peaceful resolution, reconciliation, and healing within the church.

13 February 2019

Reverend Madawo and his group held a meeting with Reverend Chikane, the President of the Apostolic Faith Mission International (AFMI), in South Africa on February 13 and 14, 2019. However, Reverend Chiyangwa was notably absent, as he was in Ethiopia at the time, while his team members were in Australia. Reverend Mapingure revealed that Reverend Chiyangwa was expected to travel to South Africa on February 25, 2019, to meet with Professor Chikane, but the purpose of his trip to Ethiopia and his team's visit to Australia remained unclear.

Analysts speculated that Reverend Chiyangwa was seeking support from regional and international presidents of the Apostolic Faith Mission in their respective countries. This move would be strategic, as it would garner him votes and influence within the AFMI presidents' meetings. With several countries having Zimbabwean presidents, securing their support would be advantageous in two ways. Firstly, they would vote in favor of his cause, and secondly, their influence abroad would inflate the numerical growth of his support base.

Moreover, when these international presidents return to Zimbabwe on vacation, they would likely side with Reverend Chiyangwa, influencing local congregants to perceive the Chiyangwa faction as the true and rightful leadership, regardless of the court's judgment. This would ultimately contribute to a significant swell in support for Reverend Chiyangwa, both locally and internationally, potentially tipping the scales in his favor within the AFMI.

This calculated move by Reverend Chiyangwa, as speculated by analysts, showcased his strategic thinking. If Reverend Madawo were to emerge victorious in court, Reverend Chiyangwa could potentially establish a parallel church, while still maintaining a legal connection to the Apostolic Faith Mission International (AFMI). With the backing of most AFMI presidents, he could leverage their influence to subtly manipulate or amend specific clauses related to associate members' privileges, effectively paving the way for his parallel church to be recognized within the AFMI framework.

This would enable Reverend Chiyangwa to maintain control over his faction, while also benefiting from the international recognition and affiliation with the AFMI. By doing so, he would have successfully navigated the legal and political landscape, ensuring the survival and potentially even the dominance of his faction within the AFMI. This move would also demonstrate Reverend Chiyangwa's ability to think several steps ahead, preparing for various outcomes and ensuring his position remains secure, regardless of the court's decision.

However, this potential acceptance of the breakaway group as an associate member by the Apostolic Faith Mission International (AFMI) raises several red flags and concerns. Firstly, it may be perceived as legitimizing the breakaway group's actions, setting a dangerous precedent for future splits and divisions within the organization. This could lead to a loss of trust and credibility in AFMI's leadership and decision-making processes, undermining the organization's authority and stability.

Moreover, allowing the breakaway group to use any similar name or logo could cause confusion among members and the public, diluting the brand and identity of the original "Apostolic Faith Mission in Zimbabwe". This could have long-term implications for the organization's reputation and ability to maintain a strong, unified presence. The decision may also be perceived as divisive, rather than promoting unity and cohesion within the organization, leading to further fragmentation and weakening of the global AFMI network.

Furthermore, the decision may set a precedent for other national churches to split and form their own organizations, potentially leading to a proliferation of breakaway groups and further divisions within the organization. This could result in a splintered and weakened AFMI, struggling to maintain its mission and values. It is crucial for AFMI to carefully consider the long-term implications of their decisions, ensuring they align with the organization's values, constitution, and mission. This includes upholding the principles of unity, cohesion, and integrity, while maintaining a strong and unified presence. AFMI must prioritize the well-being and stability of the organization, making decisions that promote unity and cohesion, rather than division and fragmentation.

16 February 2019

Rev Togara Mapingura, spokesman for Rev Chiyangwa, criticized the Madawo camp for negotiating in bad faith in an interview with NewsdzeZimbabwe, a local online news outlet. He stated that Prof Chikane had been working to break the deadlock, starting with a meeting with the Madawo faction in December 2018, followed by a meeting with Rev Chiyangwa on January 31. Prof Chikane also met with the apostolic council, 800 pastors, and their spouses from the Chiyangwa group last month as part of efforts to reunite the feuding church factions.

As a preliminary step towards dialogue, the two camps agreed to cease mudslinging and respect each other's church activities. AFM International also instructed the factions to withdraw pending court cases related to the church leadership dispute. However, Rev Mapingura expressed disappointment that the Madawo camp had blocked a Widows Single Mothers Conference (WISMO) organized by the Chiyangwa group.

The Madawo group had held their WISMO from January 30 to February 2, 2019, at Rufaro Conference Centre in Chatsworth. The Chiyangwa-led executive then scheduled their WISMO for February 7, 2019, at the same venue. However, the Madawo leadership booked the venue for another prayer meeting, aware of the scheduling conflict. On February 4, 2019, Rev Madawo obtained a High Court order to block the Chiyangwa group's WISMO, violating the agreement to respect each other's activities.

During the widows' meeting on February 7, 2019, Rev Madawo's camp, armed with the court order, disrupted the gathering, forcing Rev Chiyangwa to appeal the decision at the Supreme Court. The Supreme Court ultimately ruled in favor of Rev Chiyangwa, allowing the WISMO to proceed.

On February 8, 2019, Rev Madawo sought a stay of execution from the High Court, which was dismissed. The Chiyangwa group's widows and singles meeting proceeded under heavy police presence on Saturday and Sunday, marking the collapse of dialogue between the factions.

Rev Mapingura expressed frustration, stating, "We thought Rev Madawo was genuine, but they're plotting against us while we're trying to discuss the matter." He listed the conditions for dialogue, including withdrawing the suspension of 400 pastors, dropping court cases, and abandoning the draft constitution. "This will never happen, and it spoils the dialogue," he added.

The Chiyangwa camp is outraged that Rev Madawo will lead a Workers' Council meeting on Saturday at Rufaro Conference Centre, where the draft constitution will be adopted. Rev Madawo declined to comment on the meeting, saying, "Let's talk after February 23, 2019. We don't want our issues published in newspapers; we want to keep out of the public eye."

Despite this, Rev Madawo claimed his group was open to dialogue and met with Rev Chikane in South Africa on February 13 and 14. Rev Mapingura confirmed that Rev Chiyangwa would meet Prof Chikane in South Africa on February 25, 2019.

The AFM has been divided over the draft constitution for two years, leading to pastors quitting and starting new ministries. Violent clashes, including fist-fights, have been captured on video, raising questions about the true motives behind the fight for control of the mega church. Is it about proper governance or the love of money?

CHAPTER twelve

United in Division: Reforms Press On Regardless

On Saturday, February 23, 2019, an Extraordinary Council meeting was held at Rufaro, where the Apostolic Faith Mission (AFM) in Zimbabwe Constitution was amended and adopted. A total of 1,412 councillors were present, marking a significant milestone in the church's history.

The significant decrease in attendance at the crucial council meeting, with 1,412 councillors present compared to 3,475 on 15 September 2018, suggests a substantial shift in support. This drop of approximately 59% implies that around half of the original number of councillors had defected to the Chiangwa faction, while others had opted out of participating in the AFM in Zimbabwe Church politics altogether. This notable decline in attendance indicates a considerable erosion of support for the Madziyire faction and a fragmentation of the church's leadership.

Despite this indication of a split in support, the actual attendance numbers at each faction's national conferences held at Rufaro Conference Centre tell a different story. The Madziyire faction drew nearly double the number of attendees compared to the Chiangwa faction, indicating a significant advantage in terms of popular support.

Local vendors who sold goods and services at both conferences provided valuable insights into the numerical strength of each faction. Based on their sales and customer interactions, they reported that the Madziyire faction had a substantial lead in terms of numerical potential customers. This suggests that the Madziyire faction has a broader base of support among the church membership, which could be a crucial factor in determining the outcome of the leadership dispute.

The disparity in attendance numbers and vendor sales also raises questions about the legitimacy of the Chiangwa faction's claims to represent the majority of the church. If the Madziyire faction can demonstrate consistent numerical superiority at national gatherings, it may bolster their case for recognition as the authentic leadership of the AFM in Zimbabwe.

Back to the Amended Constitution. The amended constitution incorporated elements from the old constitution, while also introducing new provisions. Some of the key changes included the replacement of the judiciary with an Adjudicative Order, addressing concerns raised by those who had left the church. Additionally, the role of Youth Leader was elevated from the assembly to the national level, and the position of Ladies Leader, held by the wife of the pastor, was retained, provided the incumbent is able to fulfill the duties.

Other notable amendments included the setting of minimum and maximum salaries for pastors, to be paid from the consolidated revenue fund. The Confession of Faith was retained, and assemblies were allowed to retain 20% of their revenue, subject to review at the next council meeting. Furthermore, the constitution stipulated that no collections could be levied except under the specific authority of the constitution or an Act of the General National Council.

The amended constitution was declared effective from February 23, 2019, and a final version was to be presented and verified at the May 4, 2019, General National Council Meeting. These changes marked a significant step forward for the AFM in Zimbabwe, addressing internal concerns and setting a new course for the church's governance and operations.

Thus, the Apostolic Council and the Workers Council in AFM in Zimbabwe came to an end, marking the beginning of a new era with the establishment of the National Executive Board and its four main committees. These committees include the Remuneration Committee, the Delimitation Committee, the Audit and Finance Committee, and the Recruitment Committee.

The National Executive Board comprises 19 members, including the Non-Executive Chairman, who is a pastor, the President, the Deputy President, Secretary General, Treasurer General, Head of Adjudicative Order, Education Board Chairman, Social Welfare Board Chairman, National Evangelism

Leader, Legal Advisor, National Employment Board Chairman, and eight Board members, consisting of four pastors and four elders.

The Remuneration and Audit and Finance committees each have three members, while the Delimitation and Recruitment committees have six members each. Members of the National Executive Board make up most of the committee members, and individuals may serve on multiple committees based on their capabilities. This new structure streamlines governance and decision-making within AFM in Zimbabwe.

The Workers Council was replaced by the General National Council, which comprises all members of the National, Provincial, and Assembly Executive Boards. This means that all pastors and elders aged 65 and below are part of the General National Council.

The Provincial Executive Board has a specific composition, with a total of eleven members. This usually include two pastors, six elders, and three deacons, based on proportional calculations. The number of elders in the province determines the number of pastors and deacons to be included. In some cases, there may only be one pastor on the Board, who is the overseer and an ex-officio member of the Provincial Executive Board.

Notably, the representation of deacons is limited to at most one-third of the assembly board members and usually three members in the Provincial Executive Board. This structure aims to balance representation among pastors, elders, and deacons.

It's worth noting that the numerical growth of elders may have implications for the number of pastors on the Board in the long run, but this aspect will not be explored further here.

One of the primary grievances raised by the Chiangwa faction was the proposed replacement of the Ladies Chairwoman with a Ladies Leader who was not necessarily the pastor's wife. However, this was addressed through an amendment, clarifying that the pastor's wife is indeed the Ladies Leader, not chairlady, as the pastor already serves as the chairman of that department. This change acknowledged the vital supporting role that a pastor's wife plays in the

Ladies Department, mirroring the biblical principle of a wife being a helper to her husband, as seen in the story of Adam and Eve.

The amendment also provided for exceptional circumstances where the pastor's wife may be unable to fulfill her duties, allowing for another capable lady to assume the role. This provision ensured continuity and effectiveness in the Ladies Department while maintaining the importance of the pastor's wife's position.

Furthermore, the amendment drew parallels with the role of a first lady in a nation, who often works in support of her husband's duties without needing explicit constitutional recognition. Similarly, the pastor's wife enjoys the privileges and responsibilities of her position by virtue of her relationship with the pastor, without requiring explicit constitutional provision.

Additionally, the Chiangwa faction's departure indirectly facilitated other key changes, including the replacement of the proposed judiciary system with an Adjudicative Order. This change addressed concerns raised by those who had left the church, rendering their complaints baseless. The situation highlights that quitting is not always a solution and can sometimes result in losing one's case, as the church has since moved forward with necessary reforms.

23 March 2019

On 23 March 2019, a significant development occurred in the ongoing legal battle within the Apostolic Faith Mission in Zimbabwe (AFMZ). The two rival factions, each claiming to be the rightful leadership of the church, filed motions to consolidate two separate court cases: HC9149/18 and HC179/19. This consolidation aimed to hear both cases simultaneously, streamlining the legal process.

The first case, HC9149/18, was initiated by the Madziyire faction on 4 October 2018, against the Chiangwa faction, comprising seven individuals. The second case, HC179/19, was filed by the Anti-Reform Side on 10 January 2019, against the Reform Side. Both applications sought a court declaration affirming their respective groups as the legitimate office bearers of AFMZ.

Notably, both factions relied on the same constitution and church regulations to support their claims. Each side accused the other of violating these governing documents, underscoring the need for consolidation. By combining the cases, the court could address the core issue: determining the authentic leadership of AFMZ.

The consolidation of these cases marked a crucial step towards resolving the protracted dispute within the church. By hearing both cases together, the court could consider the arguments and evidence presented by each faction, ultimately making a comprehensive ruling on the rightful leadership of the Apostolic Faith Mission in Zimbabwe.

4 May 2919

On May 4, 2019, the General National Council convened at Rufaro, the National Conference Center of the Apostolic Faith Mission in Zimbabwe, marking a significant milestone in the church's history. Due to the concurrent National Ladies Conference, the meeting was held at the Rufaro Schools grounds, accommodating the ongoing ladies' activities at the conference center arena.

This council meeting was a follow-up to the Extraordinary Workers Council meeting held on February 23, 2019, where the amended constitution was accepted and adopted. The gathering aimed to verify, approve, and sign the amended constitution as the complete and official document governing the church.

The verification process ensured that all members were in agreement with the amended constitution, and the approval process solidified its acceptance. The signing of the document marked its formal adoption, making it the supreme governing document for the Apostolic Faith Mission in Zimbabwe. This milestone signified the church's commitment to embracing change and adapting to its evolving needs, while maintaining its core values and principles.

This day marked a significant milestone, as it signaled the commencement of the five-year term for all elected boards and committees across various levels, ranging from assembly to national. This includes the National Advisory Council, which plays a crucial role in providing guidance and support to the church's leadership.

As outlined in the constitution, the election cycle for these boards and committees is staggered, ensuring a smooth transition and maintaining continuity. The Assembly Executive Boards and their committees will hold their next elections in June, followed by the Provincial elections in July, and culminating in the General National Council elections in August, all within the fifth year of the term.

This cycle will repeat every five years, with elections scheduled for:

- June: Assembly level
- July: Provincial level
- August: National level

This structured approach ensures that the church's leadership is regularly refreshed, bringing new perspectives and ideas, while also maintaining stability and consistency in its governance. The constitution's provisions for regular elections demonstrate the church's commitment to accountability, transparency, and democratic principles.

4 July 2019

The invitation letter from the AFMI dated 4th July 2019 was emailed to Rev Amon Dubie Madawo, as was to all Church's Presidents in member countries. The council for the Presidents was slated for 19 August 2019 at Kenyatta University.

AFMI's action implied that they had recognized Rev Madawo as the President of AFM in Zimbabwe, although Rev C Chiangwa had been elected into the same of on 20 October 2018, while Rev Madawo was elected to replace Dr Madziyire on 3 November 2018.

Although Rev C Chiangwa was not invited, or maybe he was verbally invited, he was there in Kenya

10 July 2019

On July 10, the Chiangwa vs Madziyire consolidated court case was finally heard in the High Court, before Judge Mangota, as an opposed application, with

Adv F Girach, for the applicants, and Adv L Uriri, for the respondents, and became it was a Consolidated case, on the flip side of it, the Chiangwa side, Adv T'Magwaliba was for the applicants, and Adv F Girach, for threspondents.

Case number HC 9149/18 by the Reform Side, was the flip side of HC 179/19 by the Anti-reform side.

Judgment was reserved indefinitely.

15 July 2019

On July 15, 2019, Pastor MG Mahlobo, secretary-general of AFM International, addressed a letter to the Apostolic Faith Mission in Zimbabwe, led by Rev Madawo, highlighting constitutional breaches that threatened the reputation of the international church. The letter emphasized that the Zimbabwean church's adoption of a new constitution with a Confession of Faith differing from AFM International's was tantamount to defining itself outside the international organization's parameters.

Pastor Mahlobo pointed out that this action constituted a breach of constitutional requirements, specifically Clause 2 of the AFM International constitution, which states:

- Acceptance of and adherence to the common Confession of Faith of the Apostolic Faith Mission International (Article 3 of this constitution)

- Acceptance of the constitution of the AFM International

- Submission of the constitution and any rules and regulations governing the said church

Furthermore, the clause requires member churches to notify AFM International of any constitutional changes by submitting a copy of their new constitution, indicating the relevant changes made.

The letter urged Rev Madawo to consider the consequences of his actions and the potential reputational damage to the integrity and witness of AFM International. Pastor Mahlobo expressed hope that God would enable Rev Madawo to see the gravity of the situation and take corrective action to avoid further damage.

A comparative analysis of the two letters written by Rev. Mahlobo, the earlier one on September 6, 2018, and the current one, reveals a distinct difference in tone. The later letter appears to align with Rev. Chiangwa's claim that the Madziyire faction had seceded from the church by accepting constitutional reforms. However, upon closer examination, Rev. Mahlobo's accusation seems tenuous, as the changes to the Confession of Faith were merely semantic, involving subtle differences in wording and emphasis, rather than any substantial alterations to the church's fundamental beliefs.

For instance, the original Confession of Faith might state, "In the Beginning, God created the heavens and the earth," whereas the revised version might read, "In the beginning, God created heaven and earth." While the two phrases convey similar meanings, the altered wording could be interpreted differently, potentially leading to disparate understandings of the church's core beliefs.

In this context, Rev Mahlobo's assertion that the Madziyire faction had strayed from the original constitution holds merit. Nevertheless, his tone suggests an underlying motive or concern that goes beyond mere semantic differences. The letter's language and emphasis imply a deeper issue, potentially related to the power dynamics or ideological divisions within the church. Rev Mahlobo's tone may be seen as cautionary, urging the Madziyire faction to reconsider their actions and reconcile with the original constitution to avoid further divisions and reputational damage to the church.

On the other hand, Rev. Mahlobo's actions could be perceived as favoring the Chiangwa faction, although there is limited evidence to support this claim. However, with the upcoming AFMI elections, where Rev. Frank Chikane will not be a candidate, the outcome may shed more light on Rev. Mahlobo's true intentions. If the election results mirror the situation in AFM Zimbabwe, where the Secretary General assumed the presidency, it may become clear that Rev. Mahlobo's actions were indeed biased towards the Chiangwa faction. This could lead to significant consequences, such as the Chiangwa faction replacing AFM Zimbabwe's representation within AFMI or the creation of a new, unified national church comprising both factions. Alternatively, a new setup might be established to accommodate Chiangwa's group. If this occurs, it would be a precedent-setting event within AFMI, potentially paving the way for similar developments in other countries.

Following the receipt and consideration of Rev. George Mahlobo's letter, the Madziyire faction may choose to re-examine the Confession of Faith section of the amended constitution. In an effort to address Rev. Mahlobo's concerns and potentially alleviate tensions, they may decide to revise the Confession of Faith to align perfectly with the AFMI's version, adopting a word-for-word match. However, this raises several questions: Would this revision be enough to satisfy Rev. Mahlobo and the AFMI, or would they continue to dispute the legitimacy of the Madziyire faction's leadership? Would this change be seen as a genuine attempt at reconciliation or merely a strategic move to appease the AFMI? Furthermore, would the Chiangwa faction, which has been aligned with Rev. Mahlobo's views, accept this revision and work towards reunification, or would they persist in their claims of legitimacy? Ultimately, the outcome of such a revision would depend on the motivations and actions of the various parties involved, and whether they are truly committed to finding a resolution to the ongoing conflict.

One commentator astutely observed that Rev. Mahlobo's letter could be seen as advantageous to the Madziyire faction, as it provides them with an opportunity to rectify any perceived flaws in their constitution and align with AFMI's requirements. By doing so, they can strengthen their position and demonstrate their commitment to unity and compliance. Moreover, if the Supreme Court upholds their High Court victory, the AFMI would be left with no further grounds to dispute the legitimacy of the Apostolic Faith Mission in Zimbabwe's leadership. This would effectively neutralize any claims of illegitimacy and solidify the Madziyire faction's position.

On the other hand, Rev. Mahlobo's letter can also be seen as a tacit acknowledgement by the AFMI that the Madziyire faction is, in fact, the authentic AFM in Zimbabwe. By engaging with them and outlining the necessary corrections, the AFMI is implicitly recognizing their authority and legitimacy. If the AFMI had truly believed the Chiangwa faction to be the genuine AFM in Zimbabwe, they would have likely ignored the Madziyire faction's claims and maintained their support for Chiangwa's group. Instead, Rev. Mahlobo's letter serves as a confirmation that the AFMI recognizes the Madziyire faction as the rightful leadership, and is willing to work with them to resolve any outstanding issues.

CHAPTER thirteen

The Fall of the Anti-reformists

On August 1, 2019, the Apostolic Faith Mission (AFM) in Zimbabwe made a significant commitment to reverse its amendments to the Confession of Faith, ensuring a word-for-word alignment with the Apostolic Faith Mission International (AFMI) version. This decision was prompted by the threat of expulsion from the international mother organization if the Zimbabwean chapter failed to conform to the AFMI's Confession of Faith. In a remarkable admission, the AFM in Zimbabwe revealed that it had been operating without guidance from the AFMI constitution. This development was reported by Daniel Nemukuyu, Investigations and Special Reports Editor at The Herald. By reversing its amendments, the AFM in Zimbabwe aims to maintain its affiliation with the international organization and avoid potential expulsion.

As previously discussed, the discrepancy in the Confession of Faith between AFM in Zimbabwe and AFMI was solely a matter of wording, with no significant differences in doctrine or belief. However, it was astute of AFMI to bring this to the attention of AFM in Zimbabwe, as even minor variations in language can have far-reaching implications. A simple miswording or subtle difference in phrasing can alter the meaning and interpretation of a statement, leading to potential misunderstandings or miscommunications. For instance, the distinction between "a truth" and "the truth" may seem minor, but it can convey vastly different ideas. "A truth" implies one of many truths, whereas "the truth" suggests a singular, absolute truth. Such nuances in language can have significant effects on the understanding and application of the Confession of Faith, making it essential for AFMI to ensure consistency and accuracy across all its affiliate organizations. By addressing this discrepancy, AFMI demonstrates its commitment to maintaining unity and clarity in its beliefs and practices.

19 August 2019

The AFMI Conference in Kenya provided an opportunity for the organization to address the developments in Zimbabwe. Rev. Madawo, who had been invited to attend the Council of Presidents on August 19, 2019, at Kenyatta University, declined participation but requested to be allowed to attend as an observer, citing instability in the church at home. According to a report in the Zim Morning Post on August 27, 2019, Rev. Madawo asked AFMI to relegate Zimbabwe's status to observer only, given the church's internal turmoil.

In a letter to AFMI, Rev. Madawo explained the reasons behind their decision to temporarily withdraw from participating in the Council:

"This letter serves to inform you that, as the AFM in Zimbabwe leadership, we have decided to recuse ourselves from participating in the Council for the following reasons:

1. Our internal affairs (i.e., the church in Zimbabwe) are not in order.

2. The AFMI is already engaged with this matter.

3. The issue is currently pending before the courts in Zimbabwe."

By recusing themselves, Rev. Madawo and the AFM in Zimbabwe leadership acknowledged the need to prioritize resolving their internal conflicts and legal issues before engaging in international gatherings.

21 August 2019

On Wednesday, August 21, 2019, a significant event occurred at the AFMI Conference in Kenya, where Rev. Frank Chikane, the President of AFMI, publicly introduced Rev. Madawo as the President of the Apostolic Faith Mission in Zimbabwe. This introduction was a clear recognition of Rev. Madawo as the legitimate and official leader of the church in Zimbabwe, at least until the pending court judgment was finalized.

By acknowledging Rev. Madawo's leadership, Rev. Chikane and AFMI demonstrated their support for his presidency, despite the ongoing disputes and court cases. This move can be seen as a strategic decision to maintain unity and stability within the organization, while also respecting the legal processes underway in Zimbabwe.

It is worth noting that this recognition by AFMI's President holds significant weight, as it reinforces Rev. Madawo's position and authority within the international organization. However, the caveat "pending the court judgment" highlights that the final outcome of the legal proceedings could still impact the leadership structure of the AFM in Zimbabwe.

Rev. Frank Chikane is a renowned South African cleric, author, and anti-apartheid activist, born on January 3, 1951, in Bushbuckridge, South Africa. He pursued his theological studies at the University of Natal and later earned a Ph.D. in theology from the University of South Africa. Chikane's unwavering opposition to apartheid led to his arrest and detention on multiple occasions. Throughout his illustrious career, Chikane has held various leadership positions within the church. He served as the President of the Apostolic Faith Mission International (AFMI) from 1996 to 2009 and again from 2013 to 2019. His tenure was marked by a commitment to promoting unity and social justice within the church and beyond. In addition to his church leadership, Chikane is a prolific author, having penned several books, including "No Life of My Own" and "The Truth Hurts". These works offer a glimpse into his experiences as an anti-apartheid activist and his perspectives on faith, justice, and leadership. Chikane's contributions to the fight against apartheid and his leadership in the church have been recognized through various awards and honors. Following South Africa's transition to democracy, he served as a special advisor to former President Thabo Mbeki and remained involved in initiatives promoting reconciliation and social justice.

At present, Rev. Frank Chikane remains actively engaged in various church and social justice endeavors, having transitioned to the role of President Emeritus of the Apostolic Faith Mission International (AFMI) following his stepping down as President, effective from the Kenya Conference of AFMI. His legacy as a champion of justice, equality, and faith continues to inspire and influence generations of South Africans and beyond.

With this distinguished background, Dr. Frank Chikane's introduction of Rev. Amon Dubie Madawo as the President of the AFM in Zimbabwe was a deliberate and informed decision. While the court judgment may bring future developments, at present, Rev. Madawo is indeed the recognized President of the Apostolic Faith Mission in Zimbabwe, not Rev. C. Chiangwa.

4 September 2019

On September 4, 2019, Justice Mangota delivered the judgment on the consolidated case numbers HC 9149/18 and HC 179/19, ruling in favor of the Madziyire faction. After carefully considering all the circumstances of both cases, Justice Mangota stated that Madziyire had successfully proven his case on a balance of probabilities. In contrast, Chiangwa failed to meet the required standard, unable to prove his case on a balance of probabilities.

Justice Mangota's ruling led to the granting of HC 9149/18 as prayed, while HC 179/19 was dismissed with costs. This outcome marked a significant victory for the Madziyire faction, validating their claims and reinforcing their position within the church. The judgment brought clarity to the longstanding dispute, providing a sense of closure and resolution for the parties involved. The court's decision underscored the importance of evidence-based claims and the need for parties to meet the required legal standards in order to succeed in their cases.

September 16, 2019

According to an article by Daniel Nemukuyu, Investigations and Special Reports Editor for The Herald, the Apostolic Faith Mission in Zimbabwe (AFM), led by Pastor Amon Madawo, acknowledged errors in the hasty amendment of their constitution and committed to reversing all the changes to align with AFM International's constitution. Pastor Brighton Tembo stated that AFM in Zimbabwe was willing to reverse their actions and adopt the AFM International Confession of Faith verbatim.

However, upon closer examination, it appears that the reversal only pertained to the Confession of Faith, not all the changes as reported. In reality, only the Confession of Faith was revisited and rectified. Notably, the changes to the Confession of Faith had no adverse impact on the Bona Fide AFM in Zimbabwe, and no councilors would have voted against them. In fact, the changes worked in favor of the AFM in Zimbabwe, led by Rev Madawo, as AFM International could no longer raise constitutional objections against the local church.

This move by AFM International can be seen as a constructive step, rescuing AFM in Zimbabwe from potential harm. By aligning with AFM International's constitution, AFM in Zimbabwe demonstrated a commitment to unity and cooperation. The reversal of the Confession of Faith changes signified a willingness to compromise and find common ground, ultimately strengthening the relationship between AFM in Zimbabwe and AFM International.

27 May 2021

On the eve of the highly anticipated Supreme Court judgment, the appellants, representing the Chiangwa faction, stood at a critical crossroads. The next day's ruling would either overturn the Madziyire faction's previous High Court victory, potentially shifting the balance of power in their favor, or solidify the Madziyire faction's control over the Apostolic Faith Mission in Zimbabwe, leaving the appellants' claims in tatters.

As we now know, the appellants ultimately lost their appeal, allowing the Madziyire faction to consolidate their hold on the church. In retrospect, it is essential to conduct a post-mortem analysis of the events leading up to this pivotal moment, examining the strategic decisions and circumstances that contributed to the appellants' defeat.

By scrutinizing the developments on the day before the Supreme Court judgment, we can gain valuable insights into the factors that influenced the outcome, including any potential missteps, miscalculations, or unforeseen events that may have impacted the appellants' chances of success. This examination will provide a deeper understanding of the complex dynamics at play and shed light on the critical moments that shaped the fate of the appellants and the future of the Apostolic Faith Mission in Zimbabwe.

First and foremost, the majority of technical issues raised by the Chiangwa faction were ineffective in resolving the dispute between the parties, rendering them essentially worthless. Their arguments often failed to benefit even themselves, let alone the opposing Madziyire faction. In fact, these arguments frequently backfired, ultimately working to the advantage of the opposing faction.

The core argument presented by the Chiangwa faction was that the Madziyire faction had violated the church's constitution. However, the Madziyire faction countered with similar claims against the Chiangwa faction. Consequently, the constitution will be scrutinized to determine which faction has the legitimate claim to leadership. The outcome will largely depend on which faction is found to have committed more severe violations of the church's constitution and regulations.

In essence, the dispute resolution process will involve a thorough examination of the alleged constitutional violations by both factions. The faction found to have committed more egregious violations will forfeit their claim to leadership, allowing the other faction to prevail.

This approach ensures that the leadership of AFM in Zimbabwe is determined by adherence to the church's governing documents, rather than by technicalities or procedural maneuvering. While procedure plays a crucial role in legal matters, the primary focus will be on upholding the principles and rules enshrined in the church's constitution and regulations. By doing so, the outcome will reflect a genuine commitment to the church's governance framework, rather than mere procedural compliance.

If a party has successfully mastered both procedural compliance and adherence to the principles and rules enshrined in the church's constitution and regulations, it will possess a significant advantage. This dual proficiency will not only demonstrate a thorough understanding of the church's governance framework but also showcase a commitment to upholding its core values and principles, thereby strengthening their position in the dispute resolution process.

By asserting that Madziyire's term of office ended on 28 April 2018, Chiangwa inadvertently acknowledged that his own term of office also expired on the same date. Consequently, his tenure could not extend beyond 28 April 2018. As of that date, he ceased to be the deputy president of the church. Moreover, even if the constitution had granted the Deputy President the authority to convene a Workers Council (which it does not), Rev Chiangwa would have lacked the mandate to do so after 28 April 2018. Therefore, when he convened the Workers Council on 22 September 2018, he did so as the leader of a rival movement, rather than in his former capacity as Deputy President of the Apostolic Faith Mission in Zimbabwe. This distinction undermines the legitimacy of the Workers Council and Chiangwa's subsequent claims to leadership.

The crux of this argument is that Chiangwa failed to think through the implications of his statement that Madziyire's term had expired, and in doing so, inadvertently revealed a glaring inconsistency in his own position. By claiming Madziyire's term ended on 28 April 2018, Chiangwa implicitly suggested that his own term was somehow exceptional, extending beyond the usual limits to expire on 22 September 2018, a full five months later. This lack of clear thinking and logical consistency undermines Chiangwa's argument and raises questions about his true intentions and understanding of the church's governance structure.

Furthermore, in a contradictory move, Rev Chiangwa asserts that he took on the role of chairperson of the Interim Committee on 22 September 2018, yet in a letter dated 26 September 2018, addressed to the Madziyire faction's office bearers, he signed off as the Deputy President of the AFM in Zimbabwe Church. This is puzzling, as he had previously claimed that his extraordinary term as Deputy President had expired on 22 September 2018. By signing the letter with a title he claims to have relinquished four days prior, Rev Chiangwa exposes a glaring inconsistency in his narrative, raising further questions about his legitimacy and understanding of the church's leadership structure.

In another anomaly, Rev Chiangwa's argument hinges on the claim that the Madziyire faction's amendments to the constitution effectively severed their ties to the Apostolic Faith Mission in Zimbabwe, prompting his faction to adhere to the original, unamended constitution. However, a closer examination reveals a striking inconsistency: neither the unamended constitution nor its accompanying regulations grant Rev Chiangwa the authority to convene a national workers council, such as the one he organized on 22 September 2018. By doing so, Rev Chiangwa ironically violated the very constitution he purported to uphold, undermining his own legitimacy and revealing a disconnect between his actions and the governing documents he claims to champion.

In stark contrast to the 15 September 2018 meeting, which was convened in compliance with a court order (case number HC 4756/18), the 22 September 2018 gathering was deliberately orchestrated with scant notice, violating the constitution's stipulation of a minimum 30-day notice period. Moreover, the meeting was presided over by Rev Enos Manyika, a retired president who lacked the constitutional authority to chair such a meeting. This is particularly egregious given the faction's professed commitment to upholding the unamended constitution, which they claim to champion. By flouting the very rules they purport to defend, the faction's actions betray a glaring disconnect between their words and deeds.

A closer examination of the anomalies reveals further discrepancies. The appointment of four Interim office bearers on 22 September 2018, and the subsequent appointment of 26 provincial overseers on 26 September 2018, flagrantly contravene the constitution's explicit stipulation that these positions are to be filled through electoral processes. If the Workers Council is claimed to have appointed the four executive members, it remains unclear who appointed the overseers four days later, as there is no constitutional provision for such appointments. This blatant disregard for the constitution's electoral requirements is particularly striking given the faction's accusations that the Madziyire faction had disregarded the same constitution. By unilaterally appointing officials, the faction has itself breached the very constitutional principles it claims to uphold.

Loopholes in the affidavits submitted to the High Court were uncovered, revealing a trail of inconsistencies. Upon closer inspection, it became apparent that the documents were mass-produced, with individuals simply filling in the blanks. To mention a few discrepancies in the affidavits, a staggering 72 affidavits contained identical information, while another 8 displayed the same content, suggesting a "copy-paste" approach. This tactic aimed to create the illusion of widespread discontent among church members regarding the September 15, 2018 meeting's outcome, and to justify the convening of the September 22, 2018 meeting. However, the majority of the affidavits failed to meet the legal requirements for validity, potentially rendering the entire effort null and void. The lack of authenticity and individuality in the affidavits raised serious concerns about their credibility and the motivations behind their submission, suggesting a coordinated attempt to deceive the court rather than a genuine expression of concerns from church members.

It is deeply troubling when those who are entrusted with spreading the Gospel and fulfilling the Great Commission find themselves in need of fervent prayers for their own spiritual redemption, rather than being the ones to offer guidance and support to others. This role reversal is a stark reminder that even those who are called to lead and minister to others can sometimes lose their way and require strong prayers and support to overcome their own spiritual struggles.

An affidavit is a solemn declaration, typically accompanied by a sworn oath, invoking God as a witness to the truth of one's statements. The High Court judge aptly referenced Matthew 27:74, which highlights the gravity of taking an oath, as it essentially invokes a curse upon oneself if one bears false witness. The judge astutely observed that the analyzed affidavits ironically bear false witness against themselves, undermining their own credibility. This is particularly egregious, as these affidavits were purportedly sworn to by individuals who claim to be believers and members of the church. As such, the judge ominously noted that the biblical principle outlined in Matthew 27:74 will ultimately hold the perpetrators of falsehood accountable for their actions.

The 399 affidavits, purportedly sworn by pastors, elders, administrators, and deacons, represent a fraction of the 1,569 councilors that Rev Chiangwa claimed attended the 22 September 2018 meeting, which he used to dispute Madziyire's assertion of 3,475 attendees. Notwithstanding the conflicting claims, a significant issue remains with the majority of the 399 affidavits themselves, which lack credibility and raise serious concerns about their validity. This undermines the reliability of the evidence presented and casts a shadow over the entire process.

Given the numerous discrepancies and anomalies uncovered in the 399 affidavits, it is highly unlikely that Rev Chiangwa and his team's appeal case will withstand scrutiny. The sheer volume of irregularities, including the lack of authenticity, inconsistencies, and unexplained similarities, severely undermines the credibility of the evidence presented. Furthermore, the fact that these affidavits were purportedly sworn by church leaders, including pastors, elders, administrators, and deacons, raises serious concerns about the integrity of the process and the motivations behind the submissions.

In light of these findings, it is reasonable to question the validity of the entire appeal, and it is likely that the court will take a dim view of the attempt to deceive. The discrepancies and anomalies are too numerous and too glaring to be ignored, and it is unlikely that Rev Chiangwa and his team will be able to provide satisfactory explanations for these irregularities. As such, their appeal case appears to be built on shaky ground, and it is unlikely to "hold water" under judicial scrutiny.

Indeed, the biblical principle outlined in Matthew 27:74, which warns of the consequences of bearing false witness, may ultimately catch up with those who have resorted to deceitful means, as Justice Mangota astutely predicted when handing down his judgment. The judge's prescient words serve as a stark reminder that the legal system, while imperfect, is designed to uncover truth and hold individuals accountable for their actions.

As the appeal case unfolds, it is likely that the court will scrutinize the evidence and testimony presented, and the numerous discrepancies and anomalies will be brought to light. When the dust settles, those who have engaged in dishonest tactics may find themselves facing not only legal repercussions but also the weight of their own conscience, as the words of Matthew 27:74 echo through the halls of justice.

The prediction by Justice Mangota serves as a warning that the consequences of dishonesty can be far-reaching, extending beyond the confines of the courtroom to impact one's personal and professional reputation, relationships, and even spiritual well-being. As the saying goes, "the truth will out," and those who have chosen to deceive may ultimately face the consequences of their actions.

CHAPTER fourteen

Divine Justice Exposed: Unraveling the Web of Deceit

On May 28, 2021, a three-judge appeal bench consisting of Justices Susan Mavangira, Lavender Makoni, and Samuel Kudya dismissed the appeal filed by Bishop Chiangwa and his group, comprising Amon Chinyemba, Nathan Nhira, Shepherd Sebata, Donald Mdoni, Arthur Nhamburo, and M Mashumba. The court ruled that the Chiangwa group lacked legal standing to seek recognition of their leadership in the High Court, as their claim was based on a void meeting held on September 22, 2018. This meant that all actions taken by the group since September 22, 2018, were deemed illegal.

In contrast, the group led by Bishop Amon Dubie Madawo, comprising Rev Amon Dubie Madawo, Aspher Madziyire, Munyaradzi Shumba, Tawanda Nyambirai, Clever Mupakaidzwa, Briton Tembo, and Christopher Chemhuru, had the legal standing to challenge the validity of the September 22, 2018, meeting. The appeal court upheld the High Court's judgment, affirming the legitimacy of the Madziyire faction, also known as the Reform Side, as the authentic Apostolic Faith Mission in Zimbabwe.

This ruling brought clarity to the long-standing dispute within the church, validating the leadership of Bishop Madawo's group and nullifying the actions of the Chiangwa group. The court's decision reinforced the importance of adhering to proper procedures and respecting the rule of law within religious organizations.

Following the court judgment, Rev Madawo addressed the congregation, stating that the legitimate leadership of the church would follow due process in implementing the court's orders, including managing places of worship and recovering control of church assets. He urged members to remain calm and not take matters into their own hands.

In contrast, as reported by Nyore Madzianike and Joseph Madzimure of Nehanda Radio on May 29, 2021, the Chiangwa faction, led by Rev. Chiangwa, appeared determined to continue their resistance. Dr. Nathan Nhira, the faction's secretary-general, announced that they were considering taking legal measures to maintain control of church property, pending advice from their lawyers. Nhira conceded that they had lost control of the church but vowed to continue fighting for their place within the organization, emphasizing that their primary concern was now the control of church assets, which they claimed was not addressed in the Supreme Court judgment.

Nhira encouraged members to remain in occupation of church premises and to continue using the church's name and logo. He stated that their structures at national, provincial, and assembly levels would remain in place, and their elected and appointed leaders would continue in their roles. Additionally, he announced plans to reconstitute themselves, maintaining their affiliation with AFM International until formally excluded, at which point they would establish their own international forum and design a new logo.

The Chiangwa faction's stance indicates a willingness to continue their dispute, despite the court's ruling, and to explore alternative measures to maintain their influence within the church.

However, what Dr. Nathan Nhira appeared to overlook was that the Supreme Court's ruling was an opposed appeal case, which had previously been settled in the High Court. The three-member bench of the Supreme Court upheld the High Court judgment in its entirety, without any modifications or exceptions. Specifically, the Chiangwa faction's appeal was dismissed with costs, incurring additional expenses beyond the initial High Court costs. This outcome meant that the original ruling made by Judge Mangota in the High Court, which favored the Madziyire faction, remains standing and unchanged. The Supreme Court's decision effectively reinforced the initial judgment, solidifying the Madziyire faction's legal victory and leaving the Chiangwa faction to bear the added financial burden of the appeal.

The Chiangwa faction had appealed for a ruling that would restrict the respondents (Madziyire faction) from using the name of the fifth applicant (Apostolic Faith Mission in Zimbabwe) without authorization, and from accessing or utilizing any assets or properties belonging to the fifth applicant. They also sought an order compelling the respondents to relinquish all properties belonging to the fifth applicant that were in their possession or control. Furthermore, they requested that the Sheriff of Zimbabwe or their deputy be authorized to seize and return any properties or assets belonging to the fifth applicant if the respondents failed to comply.

Notably, the Madziyire faction had already secured a victory on these matters in the High Court, and the Supreme Court upheld this judgment, dismissing the Chiangwa faction's appeal. This outcome suggests that the Chiangwa faction sought a discriminatory application of the law, where they would benefit from its provisions while restricting the Madziyire faction's rights. This inconsistency is reminiscent of Rev. Chiyangwa's earlier expectation that Rev. Madziyire's term ended on April 28, 2018, while his own term was extended to September 22, 2018. This disparity highlights the faction's apparent desire for selective application of rules and regulations to suit their interests.

The court order subsequently provided explicit instructions, outlining specific actions that were permitted and prohibited, thereby clarifying the expectations and obligations of the parties involved.

It is alarming to observe that in a high-profile consolidated court case, where the roles of applicant and respondent are reversed, the same side exhibits identical flaws in both capacities. This phenomenon raises suspicions and suggests a lack of integrity or potential manipulation.

In a criminal case, such consistency in flaws would likely lead investigators to focus on that party as the prime suspect. The repetition of mistakes or oversights when switching roles from respondent to applicant implies a deliberate attempt to obscure the truth or influence the outcome. This pattern of behavior undermines the integrity of the legal process and warrants closer scrutiny. It is essential to examine the motivations and actions of the party exhibiting these flaws to ensure a fair and just outcome.

Furthermore, this situation highlights the importance of vigilant oversight and robust checks and balances in legal proceedings. The court's attention to detail and commitment to fairness are crucial in preventing the manipulation of justice.

In the context of the Apostolic Faith Mission in Zimbabwe (AFMZ) court case, this phenomenon is particularly concerning, given the significance of the dispute and the potential consequences for the organization's governance and stability.

A complex web of deceit and duplicity appears to have been woven within the Apostolic Faith Mission in Zimbabwe (AFMZ), with individuals potentially playing a dangerous game of running with the hares and hunting with the hounds. The presence of a double agent or mole has led to suspicions of deceit and manipulation, as evidenced by the numerous loopholes overlooked in legal documents and the failure of learned individuals to detect these inconsistencies.

This scenario implies a deliberate attempt to obscure the truth or influence the outcome, threatening the integrity and stability of the Chiangwa faction. The fact that the faction's flaws have persisted, without learning from multiple mistakes, raises questions about the presence of a deliberate saboteur.

This phenomenon is not unprecedented, as similar events have occurred throughout history. The King of Syria's predicament in 2 Kings 6:11 serves as a notable example, highlighting the age-old problem of infiltration, espionage, and betrayal.

However, it is also possible that the situation may not be solely attributed to human actions. As in the King of Syria account, the Lord's hand may be at work, orchestrating events to bring about justice or expose wrongdoing. The presence of a mole or traitor may be a physical manifestation of this divine intervention.

Moles, by their nature, operate stealthily and craftily, making them difficult to detect. Their actions can have far-reaching consequences, damaging the reputation and stability of organizations.

Ultimately, this situation serves as a reminder of the importance of vigilance, transparency, and accountability in leadership. The manipulation of circumstances and exploitation of trust can have severe consequences, emphasizing the need for integrity and honesty in all aspects of organizational governance.

As the biblical principle states, "Do unto others as you would have them do unto you" (Matthew 7:12). This situation also illustrates the truth of the proverb, "He who digs a pit to snare others will fall into his own craft" (Proverbs 26:27). Those who engage in deceit and manipulation may ultimately face the consequences of their own actions.

Additionally, the fundamental principle of onus in legal proceedings dictates that the party making a claim against another in a court of law bears the burden of proof to demonstrate their entitlement to the relief sought. In their appeal application, the Chiangwa faction, as appellants, egregiously overlooked this elementary principle of law, which unequivocally states that "he who alleges must prove."

The Chiangwa faction alleged that the Madziyire faction had seceded from the Apostolic Faith Mission in Zimbabwe (AFMZ), yet they failed to adduce sufficient evidence to substantiate this claim. Conversely, their own actions and conduct betrayed a stark contradiction, revealing that it was, in fact, the Chiangwa faction that had seceded from the AFMZ.

This glaring oversight and failure to discharge their burden of proof raises serious questions about the legitimacy of their claims and the veracity of their allegations. The legal principle of onus probandi, or the burden of proof, is a sacrosanct tenet of jurisprudence, and its disregard can have far-reaching consequences for the integrity of legal proceedings.

In this instance, the Chiangwa faction's inability to prove their allegations, coupled with their own demonstrable secession from the AFMZ, undermines their credibility and fortifies the position of the Madziyire faction. This turn of events highlights the importance of adhering to fundamental legal principles and the imperative of substantiating claims with concrete evidence in legal disputes.

The Chiangwa faction's claim of secession against the Madziyire faction was not a genuine appeal case, but rather a novel introduction new case, masquerading as an appeal. Astoundingly, the High Court had not previously addressed the issue of secession in any capacity, rendering the Chiangwa faction's argument fundamentally flawed.

This egregious error, coupled with the faction's and their lawyers' collective failure to grasp elementary appeal court rules, defies comprehension. It is a blunder of monumental proportions, begging the question: how could both the faction and their legal representatives overlook such basic principles?

In light of these circumstances, it is reasonable to infer that the Chiangwa faction's demise was not merely a result of human error, but rather an instance of divine intervention. The hand of God, it seems, had a role in thwarting their efforts from the outset, exposing the flaws in their argument and the folly of their actions.

This turn of events serves as a poignant reminder of the importance of diligence, attention to detail, and adherence to established legal protocols.

Moreover, it highlights the limitations of human understanding and the potential for divine influence in the pursuit of justice.

Moreover, Rev Chiangwa's actions as Deputy President demonstrated a blatant disregard for the church's constitution. On 22 September 2018, he unilaterally convened a Workers Council, despite the fact that the constitution did not empower the Deputy President to take such action. This egregious overstep was a stark violation of the church's governing document, exposing Rev Chiangwa's willingness to disregard established protocols and assume unauthorized authority.

By convening the Workers Council without constitutional mandate, Rev Chiangwa undermined the very fabric of the church's governance structure. His actions not only betrayed a lack of respect for the constitution but also revealed a troubling propensity for unilateral decision-making. This incident served as a poignant example of the consequences of prioritizing personal agenda over constitutional integrity.

Ultimately, Rev Chiangwa's disregard for the constitution came full circle, as his own actions were later cited as evidence of the illegality of his faction.

The church's constitution, which he had once claimed to uphold, ultimately became the instrument of his downfall. This serves as a cautionary tale about the importance of adhering to established governance structures and respecting the rule of law within religious organizations.

The establishment of a written constitution within the church is a deliberate and intentional act, designed to provide a clear framework for governing the affairs of its leadership and adherents. This foundational document serves as the supreme guide, outlining the organizational structure, roles, and responsibilities within the church. The constitution and accompanying regulations meticulously define the organogram, or organizational chart, of the church, ensuring clarity and precision in its governance.

Any actions, decisions, or attempts to alter the church's governance, whether by an individual or a group, that fall outside the parameters of the constitution are null and void. This means that any such attempts are deemed invalid, unenforceable, and without legal effect. The constitution stands as the ultimate authority, superseding any contrary claims or actions.

This emphasis on a written constitution ensures that the church operates with transparency, accountability, and predictability, safeguarding the rights and interests of its members. By adhering to the constitution, the church maintains its integrity, unity, and continuity, even in the face of challenges or disputes. The constitution serves as a bulwark against arbitrary decisions, abuses of power, or attempts to subvert the church's mission and values.

On a lighter note, it's worth observing that May seems to be a month of great significance for the Apostolic Faith Mission (AFM), punctuated by a series of notable milestones and events throughout the church's storied history. From pivotal moments of growth and expansion to times of trial and triumph, May has played host to a remarkable array of happenings that have helped shape the AFM into the vibrant community it is today. Whether by coincidence or design, this month has become an integral part of the church's narrative, weaving together the threads of past, present, and future.

On May 25, 1908, the AFM of South Africa was founded, laying the groundwork for the church's growth and expansion. Just two days later, on May 27, 1908, the first elections were held in the Apostolic Faith Mission of South Africa, solidifying the church's commitment to democratic principles.

Fast-forwarding to contemporary times, May continues to be a month of importance for the AFM. On May 4, 2019, the AFM in Zimbabwe adopted an amended constitution, marking a significant step forward in the church's governance and operations. This development demonstrated the church's willingness to adapt and evolve in response to changing circumstances.

Furthermore, on May 28, 2021, the Supreme Court announced its judgment, bringing closure to a prolonged and complex split within the Apostolic Faith Mission. This verdict marked the end of a challenging chapter in the church's history, allowing the AFM to move forward with renewed focus and unity.

The convergence of these significant events in May underscores the month's importance in the AFM's history and highlights the church's enduring legacy and commitment to growth, democracy, and spiritual guidance.

In conclusion, it's a paradox to consider how someone can knowingly fall into their own trap, despite being aware of its dangers. This phenomenon is distinct from self-inflicted harm, like suicide, where the individual intentionally causes harm to themselves. The biblical wisdom in Proverbs 26:27 cautions,

"He who digs a pit will fall into it himself," highlighting the spiritual principle that our actions have consequences.

When individuals pray for divine assistance while intentionally engaging in unrighteous behavior, they risk falling into their own snare. Meanwhile, their opponent may also seek God's help, but with a commitment to righteousness. In such cases, God may allow the deceitful person to become entangled in their own web of deceit, exposing their hypocrisy.

As the Bible says in Isaiah 55:11, "God will keep watch on His word until He sees it prosper." He will not be mocked or manipulated. Those who attempt to exploit God's power for their own gain will find that their cunning plans are turned against them. The wisdom of the world is no match for God's divine justice, which will ultimately prevail.

To trifle with God is to play with fire, for He is a consuming fire (Hebrews 12:29). Those who try to outsmart Him will find themselves ensnared by their own devices, while the righteous will be vindicated. As Proverbs 26:27 reminds us, those who set traps for others will ultimately fall into their own pit.

The term "Satanist" has gained widespread usage globally, particularly in Africa, implying that those labeled as such are devotees of the devil. However, it's astonishing when a fellow Christian, with whom you've shared years of worship and fellowship, publicly accuses you of being a Satanist simply because you disagree on certain issues.

This phenomenon raises fundamental questions about the nature of worship and the identity of the deity being revered. If someone calls you a Satanist, implying that you worship the devil, yet you know that your allegiance is to God, the Creator of the universe, who is being mocked and misrepresented? Is it you, the accused, or the God you worship?

The Chiangwa faction's reliance on semantic manipulation, frequently evident in audio recordings featuring their esteemed leaders, ultimately proved to be their undoing. By attempting to distort language and meaning to suit their agenda, they inadvertently exposed their own duplicity, leading to their downfall. This tactic, meant to deceive and mislead, backfired and became a crucial factor in their demise, as it may have eroded trust and credibility before the Divine and the broader church community.

By accepting and utilizing the label of "Satanist" without critically examining its implications, they inadvertently undermined their own arguments and evidence. Their defense team, comprising learned attorneys, surprisingly overlooked the glaring inconsistencies and self-incriminating statements present in the faction's initial affidavits and subsequent court filings.

This oversight ultimately led to the demise of Chiangwa's case, as the contradictions and flawed reasoning inherent in his arguments became apparent. The misapplication of the term "Satanist" and its implications regarding the object of worship served as a critical turning point, highlighting the need for precision and clarity in theological discourse and legal argumentation.

The verbal onslaught against their opponents was relentless, with the "anti-reform side" employing a wide range of tactics to discredit and demonize their adversaries. Social media platforms, leaked audio recordings, and church gatherings all served as battlegrounds for this war of words. The vitriolic rhetoric and personal attacks were so pervasive that even neutral observers and non-aligned commentators began to predict the downfall of the "anti-reform side".

Ironically, the very group they maligned and labeled as "Satanists" ultimately proved to be their undoing. By resorting to such extreme and inflammatory language, they inadvertently undermined their own credibility and weakened their case. The sheer intensity and scope of their verbal attacks only served to galvanize opposition and create sympathy for their opponents.

Furthermore, the claim that the Madziyire faction adopted a "draconian" constitution warrants scrutiny. Specifically, what aspects of the constitution were deemed draconian? Initially, the critics argued that the constitution was incompatible with the AFM International Confession of Faith. However, upon closer examination, it appears that the true concern lay not with the constitution's principles, but rather with the equalization of benefits among pastors.

A small group of well-compensated pastors felt threatened by the amended constitution, which aimed to distribute resources more evenly among their peers. They saw this move as a direct attack on their privileged status, fearing that the new constitution would "take away their bread" and eliminate their coveted packages. In essence, the label of "draconian" was a smokescreen for their own self-interest, masking a desire to maintain their exclusive advantages rather than embracing a more equitable system.

In the end, the "anti-reform side" may have had a strong argument, but their reliance on personal attacks and vitriolic rhetoric ultimately overshadowed their message and led to their downfall. Those they sought to vilify and discredit emerged victorious, their reputation intact and their position strengthened by the unwarranted and excessive attacks.

CHAPTER fifteen

The Importance of Integrity: Lessons Learnt

Matthew 18:15-17 provides a comprehensive, step-by-step guide for resolving conflicts within the church community. The process begins with a private confrontation (verse 15), where the individual addresses the issue directly with the offender. If the offender refuses to listen, the next step is to involve one or two witnesses (verse 16) to facilitate resolution. If the issue still persists, the matter is escalated to the church leadership or council (verse 17) for further guidance and mediation. Finally, if the offender continues to harden their heart and refuses to repent, the Bible advises treating them as an unrepentant person, an outsider (verse 17).

This biblical process emphasizes the importance of exhausting all internal remedies before seeking external resolution. It's not a matter of simply forgiving and forgetting without addressing the conflict; rather, it's about tackling the issue with care and diligence, following a clear procedure to ensure justice and accountability.

In the context of the dispute between the Madziyire and Chiangwa factions, this biblical principle was applied. The Madziyire faction initially sought internal resolution but eventually took the matter to civil courts on October 4, 2018, following the biblical step-by-step process. Similarly, when the Chiangwa faction filed their own application on January 10, 2018, they were also following this procedure. However, some individuals criticized the Madziyire faction for seeking external resolution, overlooking the fact that the Chiangwa faction had also taken similar action.

Ultimately, the Supreme Court ruled in favor of the sitting executive, demonstrating the effectiveness of the biblical conflict resolution process in achieving justice and resolution. This example illustrates the importance of following biblical principles in addressing conflicts, even in complex and contentious situations.

However, the aftermath of the split has been marked by a manifestation of the "sins of the flesh" listed in Galatians, including enmities, strife, jealousy, anger, disputes, dissensions, factions, and envying. The division has led to a toxic environment, with Rev Cossam Chiangwa forming his own church, AFM of Zimbabwe, and Reverend Amon Madawo leading the AFM in Zimbabwe.

According to Ian Sumner's paper, church leaders are often the primary instigators of splits, driven by personal interests and a desire for control. This leads to a culture of fear, where followers blindly obey leaders without questioning their actions or considering the spiritual implications.

The quote from Blaise Pascal rings true, as individuals commit harm with conviction, believing they are doing right. However, this highlights the importance of individual spiritual growth and understanding. Congregants should not blindly follow leaders but rather engage with Bible doctrines to make informed decisions.

Unfortunately, some church leaders exploit their followers' ignorance, leading them astray with false teachings and misguided interpretations. This can result in a toxic cycle of division, confusion, and spiritual stagnation. However, individuals have the power to break free from this cycle by taking ownership of their spiritual journey.

Rather than relying solely on leaders, it is crucial to seek guidance from the Bible, the ultimate source of truth and wisdom. By doing so, individuals can cultivate a deeper, more authentic faith, rooted in the teachings of Christ. As Colossians 2:6-8 admonishes:

"As ye have therefore received Christ Jesus the Lord, so walk ye in him: Rooted and built up in him, and stablished in the faith, as ye have been taught, abounding therein with thanksgiving. Beware lest any man spoil you through philosophy and vain deceit, after the tradition of men, after the rudiments of the world, and not after Christ."

This passage serves as a warning against the dangers of false teachings and the importance of being grounded in the faith.

By being rooted in Christ and guided by the Bible, individuals can develop a personal relationship with God that is not dependent on human leaders. This relationship enables them to discern truth from error and deception, and avoid being swayed by worldly philosophies and traditions that may lead them astray. As they delve deeper into God's Word, they cultivate a richer understanding of its teachings and how to apply them in their daily lives. This, in turn, fosters spiritual growth and maturity, marked by a heart of thanksgiving and a life that bears fruit for God's glory. Through this journey, individuals can experience the transformative power of God's Word and develop a faith that is authentic, vibrant, and unwavering.

Ultimately, taking ownership of one's spiritual journey and seeking guidance from the Bible is essential for breaking free from the toxic cycle of division and cultivating a vibrant, authentic Faith.

The issue at hand affects not only the Chiangwa faction but also the Madziyire faction, as both have been marred by deceit. While the Chiangwa side has taken it to extremes, it's essential to acknowledge that both factions have their shortcomings. Our focus on the Chiangwa faction's flaws might give the impression that we're ignoring the Madziyire faction's mistakes, but it's widely acknowledged that the latter's flaws were relatively minor compared to the former's.

A concerning aspect is that the truth remains concealed from the congregants in Chiangwa's camp, leaving them uninformed and potentially misled. This lack of transparency and honesty has contributed to the Chiangwa faction's downfall, and it's crucial to examine their actions to understand why and how they lost their way. By doing so, we can gain valuable insights into the importance of integrity, accountability, and truthfulness in leadership.

The deception and misinforming of congregants has potentially caused irreparable harm to individuals who were genuinely misled into believing false information. Many only realized the truth too late, after they had already been manipulated into speaking out against the Madziyire faction congregations, uttering words that cannot be taken back. The severity of this situation is compounded by the fact that some individuals were coerced into taking a stance against their own brethren, only to later discover the truth and feel remorseful for their actions.

This tragic sequence of events has led some to comment that the rot began at the top, with the leadership being the first to succumb to corruption. As the saying goes, "a rotten head spoils the whole fish," implying that the toxic influence of the leadership trickled down, corrupting the entire organization. This phenomenon is a stark reminder of the importance of ethical leadership and the devastating consequences of allowing deception and misinformation to spread unchecked.

The harm caused by this deception is far-reaching and multifaceted. It has resulted in emotional distress for those who were misled, causing them unnecessary anxiety, pain, and suffering. Furthermore, the deception has damaged relationships within the congregations, creating divisions and tensions that may take a long time to heal. The erosion of trust in leadership is another significant consequence, making it challenging for the recover to recover and rebuild. Ultimately, the deception has tarnished the reputation of the church as a whole, undermining its credibility and integrity in the eyes of its members and the wider community.

It is crucial for leaders to prioritize transparency, honesty, and accountability to prevent such situations from arising and to foster a culture of trust and integrity within their churches.

Although God's offices and ways are beyond human comparison, it is a well-established biblical fact that sin entered the world through the rebellious spirit of Lucifer, also known as the devil (Isaiah 14:12-15, Ezekiel 28:12-17). The conflict between God and Satan serves as a paradigm for understanding the human experience, as illustrated in various parables where God is depicted as a farmer (Matthew 13:24-30), a bridegroom (Matthew 25:1-13), or a king (Matthew 22:2-14).

Similarly, the story of humanity can be seen as having its roots in the conflicts between God and Satan. Just as Lucifer's rebellion against God led to his downfall and the introduction of sin into the world, humanity's rebellion against God's authority has led to sin and separation from God (Genesis 3:1-7, Romans 3:23).

This parallel highlights the significance of obedience, humility, and submission to God's authority, as seen in the lives of faithful individuals like Jesus Christ (Philippians 2:5-8) and the prophets (Hebrews 11:1-40). By examining the conflict between God and Satan, we can gain insight into the human condition and the importance of aligning ourselves with God's will and purposes.

The concept of a Deputy President declaring himself the president, while declaring the rightful president as suspended, has its roots in the ancient conflict between Satan and God. This struggle for power and rulership began when Lucifer, then a celestial being, allowed pride to consume him. He coveted the honor and respect bestowed upon him by other heavenly entities and sought to elevate his status to equality with God.

Lucifer's desire for self-advancement and his unwillingness to wait for God's appointed time led him to attempt to usurp God's authority. By trying to raise his seat to equal God's, Lucifer essentially believed he could surpass God at will, demonstrating a dangerous and arrogant mindset. If God had not intervened, Lucifer's actions could have led to a coup, threatening the very fabric of heaven's order.

Similarly, when a Deputy President attempts to supplant the rightful president, it echoes Lucifer's rebellious spirit. Such actions betray a desire for power and control, often driven by pride and ambition. This behavior undermines the established hierarchy and can lead to chaos and division, mirroring the consequences of Lucifer's actions in heaven. By examining the origins of this conflict, we can better understand the dangers of unchecked ambition and the importance of respecting rightful authority.

For emphasis, let's reiterate: Lucifer, one of the highest-ranking archangels, perceived himself as second-in-command to God. Although the Bible doesn't specify if there were other archangels of equal status, it's clear that Lucifer became consumed by pride and ambition. He attempted to elevate himself to a position alongside God, seeking to equal or even surpass the Most High's authority.

This parallels the situation where a Deputy, forgetting the President's superior anointing and authority, attempts to usurp power through a coup. In both cases, the desire for power and control leads to rebellion against the established order.

In contrast, David, who was anointed by God to succeed King Saul, waited patiently for the right time to assume the throne (1 Samuel 16:13, 23:2-4). He didn't resort to a coup, demonstrating respect for God's timing and authority.

However, the story of Jacob and Esau serves as a cautionary tale about the consequences of supplanting others. Jacob, who was anointed to be greater than Esau before birth (Genesis 25:23), deceived his brother to obtain the birthright (Genesis 25:29-34). Later, Jacob faced a similar situation when Laban supplanted Rachel with Leah as his wife (Genesis 29:1-30). This illustrates the principle that what we sow, we reap, and that attempting to circumvent God's order can lead to chaos and unintended consequences.

While President Dr. Madziyire, like any human leader, had his own known and unknown shortcomings, attempting to remove him through a coup was not the appropriate solution. The fact that the Deputy President, Rev. Chiangwa, issued memos and circulars on official-looking letterheads and footnotes, but not from the official office of the Apostolic Faith Mission in Zimbabwe, raises serious concerns.

This suggests that Rev. Chiangwa was operating from outside the official structures of the church, implying a clandestine and unauthorized takeover. By using fake official documentation, Rev. Chiangwa created a false impression of legitimacy, effectively masquerading as the authentic leader of the AFM in Zimbabwe. This constitutes a form of spiritual identity theft, where an individual or group assumes the identity of a legitimate organization without authorization.

In essence, Rev. Chiangwa's actions amount to an impostor coup, where he attempted to hijack the church's authority and identity for his own purposes. This undermines the principles of transparency, accountability, and trust that are essential for healthy leadership and organizational integrity. By examining the tactics employed by Rev. Chiangwa, we can better understand the dangers of manipulation and deception in leadership transitions.

While it's not accurate to directly equate the Deputy President with Lucifer, it's essential to acknowledge that all evil influence originates from Satan, who has been a deceiver since the beginning (John 8:44). Those who engage in deceitful behavior resemble their father, the devil. However, it's crucial to note that this doesn't imply the President was flawless. The leaked phone recordings revealed shortcomings on his part, but the Chiangwa faction's extreme actions ultimately led to their downfall.

This narrative focuses on examining how and why the Chiangwa faction lost both the legal and social battles. In doing so, we may overlook the Madziyire faction's flaws, but it's essential to prioritize understanding the Chiangwa faction's failures. By analyzing their actions and decisions, we can gain insight into the consequences of their choices.

It's important to recognize that both factions had their shortcomings, but this narrative aims to explore the Chiangwa faction's mistakes and how they contributed to their defeat. By doing so, we can learn valuable lessons about leadership, integrity, and the importance of accountability.

Coaxing congregants is a subtle yet insidious form of deception, akin to an advanced lie. Beguiling, though seemingly harmless, has been the catalyst for separation from God since the dawn of time, until the redemptive power of Jesus Christ intervened. The Chiangwa faction's ability to coax and mislead has led many astray, not through deliberate intent, but rather through a lack of knowledge and understanding.

Unwittingly, numerous individuals followed the Chiangwa faction, believing it to be the authentic and original Apostolic Faith Mission (AFM) in Zimbabwe. They were convinced that the Madziyire faction was the breakaway group, and some still hold this misconception today. This is a poignant illustration of the scripture that warns, "God's people are perishing for lack of knowledge" (Hosea 4:6). This lack of knowledge is not merely a lack of information, but a lack of understanding of the truth that sets us free (John 8:32).

The coaxing and manipulation by leaders, particularly pastors, have contributed significantly to this state of affairs. By presenting a distorted version of reality, they have led many down a path of deception, obscuring the truth and hindering spiritual growth. This highlights the importance of seeking knowledge, wisdom, and discernment, and the need for leaders to prioritize transparency, honesty, and integrity in their guidance.

While it's not inherently wrong to follow the Chiangwa faction and form the Apostolic Faith Mission of Zimbabwe, some congregants may have joined unknowingly due to misinformation. Before God, this could be considered a grave sin, similar to the distinction between fornication and adultery.

Fornication typically involves only God as the offended party, whereas adultery involves a third party - the spouse - and requires seeking forgiveness from them as well.

Similarly, in this situation, one cannot simply ask God for forgiveness without considering the numerous individuals who were misled into joining the new faction. Being in a place where one shouldn't be, even unknowingly, can be as harmful as sinning intentionally. While the invisible church is unified for all believers, individuals should choose their visible church affiliation willingly, not through coercion or manipulation.

In essence, congregants should be free to make informed decisions about their church membership, without being swayed by misinformation or pressure. This ensures accountability, transparency, and a clear conscience before God. By recognizing the importance of informed choice, we can promote a healthier and more authentic expression of faith within our church communities.

Although the Chiangwa faction cannot reverse the past, it's still essential to come clean and tell the truth now. This not only clears their conscience but also serves as a valuable lesson to others who may be in similar situations, demonstrating that honesty is the only path to true freedom (John 8:32).

Just as a stolen Bible would still contain the verse "You shall not steal" (Exodus 20:15), the visible church, despite its good intentions, cannot justify manipulative tactics to attract members. The Great Commission (Matthew 28:18-20) instructs us to spread Christ's teachings to the world, baptize those who believe, and make disciples. However, this should be done through genuine evangelism, not coercion or deception.

By being truthful and transparent, we can build trust and credibility, essential for effective ministry and discipleship. Let us learn from this experience and strive to uphold integrity and authenticity in our outreach efforts, remembering that true righteousness comes from living according to God's principles, not manipulating others for our own gain.

CHAPTER sixteen

The Aftermath: From Accuser to Accused

One aspect that has led many to question Rev Chiangwa's motives and character is the perceived irony in his actions. Specifically, the alleged conflicts and issues within his own church leadership have raised eyebrows, as they eerily mirror the very same concerns he previously raised against Rev Madziyire's leadership. This has led some to suggest that Rev Chiangwa's criticisms of Rev Madziyire were merely a smokescreen for his own ambitions and desire for power.

Critics argue that Rev Chiangwa's actions demonstrate a lack of self-awareness and hypocrisy, as he has been accused of perpetuating the same issues he once condemned. This perceived double standard has led to accusations that Rev Chiangwa's primary motivation is a lust for power and control, rather than a genuine desire to serve the church and its members.

Furthermore, this situation has sparked debate about the importance of accountability and introspection in leadership. If Rev Chiangwa was truly committed to addressing the issues he raised against Rev Madziyire, it is argued that he would have taken steps to ensure those same issues did not arise within his own leadership. The fact that they have, suggests a lack of sincerity in his initial criticisms and a focus on personal gain rather than the well-being of the church.

Rev C Chiangwa, President of the Apostolic Faith Mission of Zimbabwe (AFMOZ), has been in office since October 14, 2018. However, by 2024, he had not conducted the constitutional triennial elections, effectively overlapping into another three-year term without a mandate. This raises questions about his commitment to upholding the unamended constitution, as he had claimed.

Yes, Rev Chiangwa's actions appear to be a convenient excuse to consolidate power and potentially form his own church, rather than a genuine concern for constitutional adherence. Notably, he had frequently criticized Rev

Madziyire, who had served a total of five three-year terms, a tenure that was legally permissible.

Moreover, Chiangwa's failure to hold elections and his extension of his term without a constitutional mandate undermine the principles of democratic leadership and accountability within the church. This move may be seen as a power grab, rather than a genuine attempt to lead the church in accordance with its constitution.

It is essential to examine Chiangwa's actions in the context of his previous statements and the church's constitution to determine whether his claims of upholding the unamended constitution were sincere or merely a pretext for personal ambition. The consequences of his actions may have far-reaching implications for the church's unity, governance, and relationship with its members.

According to a report by Nhau Mangirazi in News-Day on January 3, 2024, a group of concerned pastors within the Apostolic Faith Mission of Zimbabwe (AFMOZ) accused Reverend C Chiangwa of obstructing elections and violating the church's constitution. The pastors pointed out that Chiangwa's tenure had expired, as he had reached the mandatory retirement age of 65, as stipulated in the church's constitution.

The ongoing infighting within AFMOZ has reportedly dampened the spirits of many members nationwide. Regina Mubaka of Chinhoyi expressed her concerns, stating, "The AFM saga is now part of the religious inheritance challenges we face locally. It drives us away from attending church." Archbishop Busani Sibanda of The United Apostolic Faith Church emphasized the importance of clear constitutions in churches, saying, "Churches must have constitutions that align with the supreme law of the land (Zimbabwe Constitution). They should clearly outline succession procedures, distinguish between church and leader ownership, and avoid ambiguity."

Isaac Chamonyonga, chairperson of the Hurungwe Pastors Fraternity, noted that unclear laws create an environment conducive to thuggery and criminal activities within churches. Mathias Tsine, secretary-general of the Federation For Indigenous Churches of Zimbabwe, observed that the church has neglected its traditional role of preaching repentance, living a Christ-like life, and prioritizing spiritual inheritance over earthly possessions and wealth.

In line with the NewsDay report, on November 13, 2023, Fatima Dangarembizi reported for Zimbabwe Situation, citing H-Metro, that the Apostolic Faith Mission of Zimbabwe (AFMOZ), a splinter group from the Apostolic Faith Mission in Zimbabwe, is on the verge of a potential split. This development stems from disagreements among church elders regarding the organization's constitution. Allegedly, Rev Cossum Chiangwa, the church's president, unilaterally amended the constitution in an attempt to maintain his position, sparking tensions.

On November 11, 2023, a meeting of Midlands-North Province members in Kadoma turned contentious as they attempted to find a resolution to prevent a split. The situation highlights the deepening divisions within AFMOZ, threatening its unity and stability.

A meeting held by the Mid-North Province on October 24, with copies sent to the president, Rev Chiangwa, and the Overseer, Rev Joel Mathe, had expressed the concerns of pastors in the region. They felt undermined by the leadership of Rev C Chiangwa, the Provincial Overseer, Rev J Mathe, and the Provincial Secretary, Rev Gutura, and requested intervention to resolve their differences.

Despite a fellowship meeting on October 23, which included Rev Chiangwa, Rev Muhamba, Rev Mutikanhi, and all pastors, the issues remained unaddressed, leaving the pastors feeling more divided than ever. The meeting had raised hopes that their concerns would be heard, but unfortunately, this was not the case.

The pastors appealed to the executive to help resolve the long-standing problem, which had been ongoing since 2019, and expressed their distress and pain in writing the letter.

The allegation that Dr. Madziyire manipulated the Apostolic Council by packing it with Overseers, who comprised over 80% of its membership, raises concerns about the concentration of power and potential abuse of authority. This is particularly noteworthy given that only six Overseers supported Rev. Chiangwa after the September 15, 2018, Extraordinary Workers Council meeting.

Ironically, President Chiangwa appears to have adopted a similar approach, as evidenced by the report on the Mid-North Provinces' complaints. According to the report, Chiangwa confided in Provincial Overseer Rev. Joel Mathe, suggesting that he may have copied Madziyire's tactics to maintain his grip on power. This scenario may have been a mirror of what's happening in all other provinces. This implies that Chiangwa's motivation for staying in office longer may be linked to the desire to preserve the lucrative positions of Overseers, who would likely retain their benefits and influence as long as he remains president.

This perpetuation of a self-serving leadership style undermines the integrity of the church's governance structure and creates an environment conducive to abuse of power. The concentration of authority in the hands of a few individuals can lead to a lack of accountability, transparency, and representation of the broader church membership. By emulating Madziyire's approach, Chiangwa risks perpetuating a cycle of authoritarian leadership that may ultimately harm the church's reputation and relationships.

Rev Chiangwa's actions can be viewed as a case of understudy gone wrong. As Deputy President to Rev Madziyire, he had the opportunity to observe and learn from his superior over several terms in the National Executive and as Deputy. It appears that Rev Chiangwa may have been taking notes on how Rev Madziyire manipulated his way to maintain power for five consecutive three-year terms. However, instead of learning from Rev Madziyire's cunning and strategic approach, Rev Chiangwa seems to have attempted to emulate his tactics without the same level of finesse.

While Rev Madziyire played the game shrewdly, using his experience and wit to maintain control, Rev Chiangwa's approach appears more careless and heavy-handed. This lack of subtlety has led to his actions being more transparent and scrutinized, ultimately exposing his own ambitions and desire for power. In contrast, Rev Madziyire's calculated moves allowed him to maintain a veneer of legitimacy, even as he consolidated his power.

This dynamic suggests that Rev Chiangwa may have misjudged the situation, underestimating the scrutiny he would face and overestimating his own ability to manipulate the system. As a result, his actions have been perceived as more overtly power-hungry, leading to criticism and backlash from within the AFM of Zimbabwe Church.

The inconsistencies during the legal battles between the Madziyire and Chiangwa factions raise questions about whether they were collective errors by the Chiangwa executive or individual actions by Rev Chiangwa himself. Similarly, it remains unclear whether the recent indefinite postponement of elections was a collective decision or an individual effort.

If the tensions within the Apostolic Faith Mission of Zimbabwe (AFMOZ) continue to escalate, leading to legal battles, Rev Cossum Chiangwa may find himself facing a similar outcome as before. Previously, while still part of the Apostolic Faith Mission in Zimbabwe (AFM), Chiangwa was involved in a legal dispute with Rev Madziyire, accusing him of unconstitutionally amending the church's constitution. However, irony has it that Chiangwa is now facing accusations of doing the same thing - unilaterally amending the constitution to extend his presidency.

The same constitution that Chiangwa claimed Madziyire had violated is now being used against him, with allegations that he has failed to honor its provisions. This raises questions about Chiangwa's commitment to upholding the church's governing document and his willingness to manipulate it for personal gain.

Moreover, the fact that Chiangwa allegedly amended the constitution for the same reasons he accused Madziyire of - to maintain his hold on power - highlights a pattern of behavior that may ultimately work against him. If the matter ends up in court, Chiangwa's actions may be seen as hypocritical and potentially illegal, leading to a loss of credibility and possibly even his position as president of AFMOZ.

And so, Rev Chiangwa's downfall in his previous dispute with Dr Madziyire can be attributed to his own actions, including his alleged manipulation of the church's constitution and his failure to uphold its provisions. If the current tensions within his new organization, Apostolic Faith Mission of Zimbabwe (AFMOZ), continue to escalate, he may find himself facing a similar outcome - defeat and loss of credibility.

The root causes of Chiangwa's previous loss, including his reliance on deception and dishonesty, are still present and may ultimately lead to his downfall once again. To avoid this fate, Chiangwa must take a different path, one of repentance and righteousness. He must shun his previous tactics of manipulation and dishonesty, and instead choose to lead with transparency, integrity, and a commitment to upholding the principles of the church.

Only through this transformation can Chiangwa hope to resolve the tensions within AFMOZ and avoid another costly and damaging dispute. By choosing to lead with righteousness and integrity, Chiangwa can create a more positive and productive environment within his organization, one that fosters growth, unity, and a deeper connection to the church's mission and values.

CHAPTER seventeen

Examining Beneath the Surface

While Rev Cossum Chiangwa is widely regarded as a good man, with a strong commitment to his faith and a passion for leading his flock, he must remain vigilant against the insidious influence of ambition. The devil often uses ambition as a tool to corrupt even the well-intentioned, leading them down a path of destruction.

In Chiangwa's case, his ambition to lead and control has already led him astray, causing him to engage in actions that are contrary to the principles of his faith. His alleged manipulation of the church's constitution and his failure to uphold its provisions are stark reminders of the dangers of unchecked ambition.

To avoid further pitfalls, Chiangwa must be mindful of the devil's wiles and ensure that his ambition is tempered by humility, wisdom, and a commitment to righteousness. He must prioritize the needs of his flock and the principles of his faith above his own desires for power and control.

By doing so, Chiangwa can fulfill his potential as a leader and a man of God, without succumbing to the corrupting influence of ambition. He can create a legacy of integrity, compassion, and wisdom, one that will inspire and uplift future generations.

It's never too late to make a change for the better, as exemplified by the thief on the cross beside Jesus Christ, who found redemption just hours before his physical death. Similarly, the Apostolic Faith Mission of Zimbabwe (AFMOZ) can still forge a positive path forward if its leaders are willing to humble themselves, be transparent with their followers, and acknowledge their true identity as a new church with a distinct mission.

AFMOZ leaders must recognize and accept that they are no longer part of the Apostolic Faith Mission in Zimbabwe (AFMZ), their former denomination. Instead, they have formed a new church, AFMOZ, with its own unique purpose and identity. There is no shame in being an associate member of the Apostolic Faith Mission International (AFMI), but it's essential to acknowledge this truthfully, without pretending to have always been part of the organization.

By embracing their true identity and being honest with their followers, AFMOZ leaders can build trust, foster growth, and create a positive future for their church. It's time for them to swallow their pride, open up, and say the truth, allowing AFMOZ to move forward with integrity and purpose.

Another factor that has raised concerns about Rev Chiangwa's intentions and character is his church's use of dual logos. On one hand, they utilize the AFMI logo, which is identical to the one employed by the Apostolic Faith Mission in Zimbabwe (AFMZ). On the other hand, they also use a distinct logo specifically designed for the Apostolic Faith Mission of Zimbabwe (AFMOZ). This dual branding has sparked questions and suspicions among many, as it appears to be a deliberate attempt to create confusion and blur the lines between the two entities.

The use of two logos has led some to wonder if Rev Chiangwa is trying to create a sense of continuity or affiliation with the original AFMZ, while also establishing a separate identity for his own faction, AFMOZ. This ambiguity has fueled concerns about his motives, with some speculating that he may be attempting to legitimize his breakaway faction by associating it with the established AFMZ brand. The dual logos have become a visible representation of the controversy surrounding Rev Chiangwa's leadership and the split within the church.

Notably, no other affiliate church of the Apostolic Faith Mission International (AFMI) uses dual logos, making Rev Chiangwa's church the sole exception. This unique practice has raised eyebrows, as it deviates from the standard branding protocol followed by all other AFMI affiliate churches. The use of two logos by Rev Chiangwa's church has become a distinguishing feature that sets it apart from the rest, fueling further speculation about his intentions and the true nature of his affiliation with the AFMI.

The logo of the Apostolic Faith Mission International (AFMI) and its affiliated churches worldwide features a distinctive design: a cross nestled within a crown, subtly tilted backwards, symbolizing the burden of the cross borne by Christ on his journey to Calvary. This iconic imagery represents the core of the Christian faith and the church's mission.

However, a striking anomaly exists in the logo of the Apostolic Faith Mission of Zimbabwe (AFMOZ), a splinter group that has broken away from the main organization. Unlike the authentic AFM churches, the AFMOZ logo displays a cross that has been reversed, appearing as a mirror image of the original design. This alteration has significant implications, as it effectively reverses the symbolism of the cross. Instead of representing the cross being carried to Calvary, the inverted design suggests that the cross is being carried away from Calvary.

The deliberate modification of the logo by the Apostolic Faith Mission of Zimbabwe (AFMOZ) leadership raises crucial questions about their underlying motivations and values. However, it is essential to note that this change was not voluntary, but rather a result of a Supreme Court order. The court's decision came after the AFMOZ lost their claim to legitimacy in the leadership of the Apostolic Faith Mission in Zimbabwe, forcing them to deviate from the traditional logo.

This alteration signals a departure from the core principles and mission of the Apostolic Faith Mission International (AFMI), which emphasizes one AFM church per occupied country. The modified logo can be seen as a visual representation of a shift in focus or a divergence from the global organization's values.

Notably, despite the altered logo and potential divergence, the AFMI has accepted AFMOZ as a full associate member. Nevertheless, it is worth acknowledging that AFMOZ's use of a similar name and logo to the authentic Apostolic Faith Mission in Zimbabwe (AFMZ) is not ideal and may cause confusion among members. A more distinct branding approach would be beneficial to avoid perpetuating misunderstandings and ensure clarity within the organization.

The Apostolic Faith Mission of Zimbabwe (AFMOZ), also known as the Chiangwa faction, has consistently engaged in deceptive practices, as evident in their court filings and ongoing church operations. This faction has been misleading its congregants by claiming equal status with the authentic Apostolic Faith Mission in Zimbabwe (AFMZ) within the Apostolic Faith Mission International (AFMI). However, according to the AFMI constitution, AFMOZ holds associate membership status, rather than full membership.

This deliberate deception creates a false narrative among AFMOZ congregants, who are led to believe that their organization enjoys the same privileges and recognition as AFMZ within the global AFMI community. Moreover, the individuals managing the AFMI website from the United Kingdom, most likely Zimbabweans, who appear to be aligned with the Chiangwa faction, are perpetuating this misinformation by falsely presenting AFMOZ as a full member, on par with AFMZ. This raises several questions, including why AFMI, a South African-based organization established in 1996, would have its website hosted in the United Kingdom. Notably, the president and secretary-general of AFMI have always been based in South Africa, making the UK website hosting decision seem unusual. This deliberate misrepresentation on the website suggests an attempt to legitimize AFMOZ's status and create the illusion of equal standing with other member organizations, such as AFMZ. This deception has significant implications, as it may mislead members, stakeholders, and the general public about the true nature of AFMOZ's affiliation with AFMI.

This orchestrated effort aims to create the illusion of two legitimate AFM branches in Zimbabwe, both supposedly equal members of AFMI. However, this is a gross misrepresentation of the facts. The AFMI has only one recognized full member in Zimbabwe, which is AFMZ. The AFMOZ's associate membership status is a clear indication of its secondary position within the organization.

This web of deception is detrimental to the integrity of the church and the trust of its members. It is essential to expose and address these falsehoods to ensure transparency and authenticity within the AFMI community.

A misleading narrative is being perpetuated by certain individuals editing the Apostolic Faith Mission International (AFMI) website, including some writers, who claim that AFMI was founded in 1908 in South Africa. This is a gross error that requires correction. In reality, AFMI is a distinct entity from the Apostolic Faith Mission (AFM) of South Africa, with a different history, structure, and purpose.

Unlike the AFM of South Africa, which is a church with its own assemblies and congregants, AFMI is not a church and does not have a congregation of its own. Instead, it functions similarly to a Football Association, which governs and oversees various clubs, but does not have its own team or players. AFMI's role is to unite and coordinate the activities of various Apostolic Faith Mission churches worldwide, providing a platform for collaboration, support, and resource sharing.

The actual founding of AFMI occurred in 1996, with Dr. Rev. Frank Chikane serving as its first and long-time president, succeeded by Rev. George Mahlobo. In contrast, the AFM of South Africa has its own president, who is not the same as the president of AFMI. This distinction highlights the separate identities and governance structures of the two entities.

It is essential to correct this misinformation to avoid confusing the public and undermining the integrity of both AFMI and the AFM of South Africa. By acknowledging their unique histories, purposes, and structures, we can foster greater understanding and cooperation within the Apostolic Faith Mission community worldwide.

If caution is not exercised, the Apostolic Faith Mission (AFMI) International may soon face severe consequences that could have been avoided. The organization appears to be compromising its values and principles to accommodate elements that are fundamentally incompatible with its core identity. This shortsighted approach may lead to irreparable damage, and by the time the repercussions become apparent, it may be too late to rectify the situation.

The AFM International is risking its spiritual integrity and potentially jeopardizing its mission by embracing what is essentially antithetical to its beliefs. When the negative consequences of this compromise begin to manifest, the organization may find itself in a precarious position, struggling to regain its footing and restore its credibility.

It is crucial for the AFM International to reassess its priorities and reaffirm its commitment to its founding principles, lest it suffer the repercussions of its own compromises. By taking a stand for its values and refusing to accommodate incompatible elements, the organization can ensure its continued relevance and effectiveness in fulfilling its spiritual mission.

The Apostolic Faith Mission International (AFMI) Council's silence on the AFM of Zimbabwe's delay of triennial elections for an entire term is perplexing, especially considering the swift condemnation of Rev Madziyire's brief delay of just a few months in 2018, which still fell within the election year. This disparity in response raises questions about the Council's impartiality and consistency in enforcing their own rules.

Furthermore, the actions of Rev Mahlobo, the AFMI general secretary who later became president, have been suspect. In 2022, he seemed to openly supported the Chiangwa faction at their debut national conference at Mufaro National Conference Center, declaring them "now" members of the AFMI. This endorsement has sparked concerns about Mahlobo's bias and potential complicity in the Chiangwa faction's actions. However, the inclusion of the term "now" in Rev Mahlobo's announcement meant that AFM of Zimbabwe had not been always a member of the AFMI.

The Bible warns that "all that has been done in the cover of darkness shall be revealed in the light" (Luke 8:17). This scripture serves as a reminder that truth and transparency will ultimately prevail, and those who have acted in secret or with deceit will be held accountable. As the situation unfolds, it remains to be seen how the AFMI Council will address the discrepancies in their handling of the two factions and whether they will take steps to restore integrity and fairness to their leadership.

Many people are perplexed as to why the Chiangwa faction didn't opt for a distinct name, instead choosing to operate under a guise that suggests continuity with the Apostolic Faith Mission International (AFMI). This decision has led to questions about the true nature of their affiliation and whether they are, in fact, a breakaway church. It appears that the Chiangwa faction was hesitant to abandon the AFM brand and culture, likely due to concerns about losing followers who are deeply invested in the organization's identity. This raises the question: what is it about the AFMI that makes it so desirable, worth sacrificing integrity? Is it the prestige, the resources, or something else entirely? The Chiangwa faction's eagerness to remain affiliated with the AFMI, despite the controversy, suggests a deep-seated dependence on the organization's reputation and influence.

Within the Apostolic Faith Mission (AFM) churches affiliated with the Apostolic Faith Mission International (AFMI), some congregants are part of the Invisible Church of Jesus Christ, just as some congregants in various other denominations or traditions are, including the Apostolic Faith Mission of Zimbabwe, even by any other name. The Invisible Church, also known as the universal church, comprises all true believers in Jesus Christ, regardless of their denominational affiliations.

In contrast, the AFMI is not even part of the visible church but rather an organization established by AFM church chapters in various countries to facilitate cooperation and resource sharing. While affiliation with the AFMI can provide benefits, it is essential to recognize its limitations and not prioritize it over one's identity in the Universal Church.

Falsifying one's status within the AFMI to feed pride is not only unnecessary but also potentially harmful. As Jesus said, "Know the Truth, and the Truth shall set you free" (John 8:32). Embracing the truth about one's identity in the Universal Church and the nature of the AFMI can bring liberation from the bondage of pride and deception.

In reality, being part of the Universal Church, known only to God, is a more profound and eternal identity than any affiliation with a human organization like the AFMI. By acknowledging and embracing this truth, individuals and churches can find freedom, humility, and a deeper connection to the body of Christ.

Upon re-examination, this narrative appears to have an unintended bias against the Chiangwa faction, which may be attributed to its scope. The initial intention was to explore the factors that contributed to the Chiangwa faction's legal defeat and decline in numerical growth. Had the focus been on the strategies employed by the winning faction, the narrative might have unfolded differently. Nevertheless, it became evident that the losing faction's shortcomings far exceeded those of the winning faction, leading to a more nuanced exploration of the Chiangwa faction's challenges.

The church belongs to Jesus Christ, and within every denomination, there exists a group of individuals who are called, chosen, and sanctified from the foundation of the world to the end of time. These individuals comprise the invisible church, known only to God. Both the visible churches, AFM in Zimbabwe and AFM of Zimbabwe, have members who are part of this universal, invisible church, and from both churches, some will fall short of the glory of God forever.

Although the Chiangwa faction lost, they still have an equal opportunity to partake in the Kingdom of God, just like the Madziyire faction. However, until both factions learn to peacefully coexist and reproduce other denominations amicably, splits will continue to occur, reminiscent to Cesarean Section births.

This is because God does not allow stagnation and will prevent a "Tower of Babel" mentality from taking hold in His Church, instead promoting growth and diversity.

In the midst of all that transpired, God remains sovereign, seated on His throne. From His perspective, there are no accidents or unexpected events - everything unfolds according to His plan. If only God's people, particularly their leaders, would learn to wait upon the Lord and align themselves with His timing, His purposes would be fulfilled effortlessly. However, because humans often fail to wait for God's perfect timing, they encounter unnecessary struggles and sufferings that could have been avoided.

In the end, both Rev. Madziyire, the President, and his deputy, Rev. Chiangwa, had significant flaws that readers should be mindful of to avoid falling into similar traps.

In contemporary Africa, particularly in democratic nations, including those with names starting with "The Democratic Republic of...", a concerning trend has emerged. As a president's term nears expiration, discussions often arise about amending the constitution, typically to extend their tenure. Regrettably, this phenomenon has also infiltrated the church, where leaders seek to prolong their stay in power.

This was the primary cause of the split in the Apostolic Faith Mission in Zimbabwe. It was only that the Madziyire faction demonstrated greater wisdom and composure in handling the situation; otherwise, the blame would have fallen on the president, as evidenced by the many leaked recordings. Church leaders must recognize that their role is to lay a foundation for their successors, enabling them to build upon and surpass their achievements. This is exemplified in the legacy of Socrates, who taught Plato, and Plato, who taught Aristotle. Each successor exceeded their predecessor's accomplishments, yet we still revere Socrates as one of the greatest philosophers in history.

In Pentecostal circles, we honor pioneers like William Joseph Seymour, John Graham Lake, and Rev. Langton Kupara, the first Black Superintendent of the Apostolic Faith Mission in Zimbabwe. Notably, these leaders did not cling to power or position. Instead, they paved the way for their successors to excel.

The concept of deputy leadership is often misunderstood. A deputy can achieve great things without being greater than their superior. Jesus Christ promised that believers would do greater works than He did, not because they would be greater than Him, but because they would build upon His foundation. This mindset allows for harmonious leadership transitions and the continued growth of the organization.

About the Author

Jaison Ndlovu, born on July 1, 1960, in Guruve, Zimbabwe, grew up in Bharamasvesve, Zhombe, Kwekwe. He is the second child and eldest son of Katazo Amos Magundwane and Resiya Chikwinya. With four sisters and four brothers, he attended Gwesela St Andrew's School, St Martin de Porres, and Ascot Secondary School for his education. He pursued salesmanship at the Union College of South Africa and Religious Studies at Ambassador Bible College. Jaison is married to Susan Ndlovu (nee Mahogo), and they have four sons and two daughters, all of whom are married. Staying at Empress in Zhombe, Zimbabwe, he is an active contributor as a blogger and editor on Wikipedia, and shares video songs and sermons on YouTube.